THE ACTION HEROINE'S HANDBOOK

Warning: The skills taught within this handbook are meant for the use of true action heroines only—not for wicked witches, female felons, or devious dames of any type. If you fall into one of these categories, put this book down immediately and slowly back away from the register. (We have inserted a traceable microchip inside the binding of this book, so do not attempt to abscond with it—we will be watching you. See that man over there? He's actually an undercover heroine. Authentic-looking bulge, don't you think?) Although the information within comes directly from highly trained professionals, we present these skills for entertainment purposes only—use this book at your own risk. Moreover, we do not assert that the information presented within is complete, safe, or accurate for the situations you may find yourself embroiled in (i.e., improvise as necessary). The authors, the publishers, and the experts within hereby disclaim any liability from any harm, injury, or damage due to the use or misuse of the information contained within this book. Finally, nothing in this book should be construed or interpreted to infringe or encourage infringement of the rights of other persons or of any state, federal, global, or universal laws. All activities described should be conducted in accordance with the law and your own good judgment—even if a coworker just stole your idea and you want to choke the life out of him with your bare thighs.

—The Authors

The
ACTION
HEROINE'S
Handbook

How to Win a Catfight,
Drink Someone Under the Table,
Choke a Man with Your Bare Thighs, and
Dozens of Other TV and Movie Skills

by Jennifer Worick and Joe Borgenicht
Illustrations by Larry Jost

QUIRK BOOKS
PHILADELPHIA

Library of Congress Cataloging in Publication Number: 2001012345

ISBN: 1-931686-68-8

Printed in The United States

Typeset in Glypha and Univers Condensed

Designed by Frances J. Soo Ping Chow

Distributed in North America by Chronicle Books
85 Second Street
San Francisco, CA 94105

10 9 8 7 6 5 4 3 2 1

Quirk Books
215 Church Street
Philadelphia, PA 19106
www.quirkbooks.com

CONTENTS

Chapter 3: Brain Skills ... 78

Chapter 4: Brawn Skills ... 122

FOREWORD

By Danielle Burgio

There was a time not so long ago when "action heroine" was an oxymoron. Sure, Bond had his female sidekicks, and yes, there'd been plenty of wisecracking, fast-talking dames on the silver screen, but no one seemed to understand that women really could do more than dance backward in high heels.

That's where I come in. As a Hollywood stuntwoman, I have been fortunate enough to have had the opportunity to actually perform the heroic stunts you see in *The Matrix: Reloaded*, *Daredevil*, *Angel,* and *Fastlane*—all of which feature the unique daring of strong, professional, and heroic women out to better the world.

In the last 30 years, there have been more and more action heroines on the big and small screens, from the original Angels all the way to Trinity, and *The Action Heroine's Handbook* is a wonderful homage to all of their astonishing exploits. Jennifer Worick and Joe Borgenicht have come up with the *real-life* instructions for living the TV and movie heroine's life—the kind of pointers a stuntwoman needs to know to perform every day on set (and off).

Based on my experience and the essential skills provided in this book, here are what I like to call the "5 Fundamental Tips of Action Heroine Survival."

Action Heroine Tip #1: Those heels are made for more than just dancing (see page 16).

Elektra may have worn heels in her everyday life from time to time, but she also knew how to run down an archenemy without missing a beat (or breaking a heel). And you'd be amazed at the amount of damage a well-placed stiletto can inflict.

Action Heroine Tip #2: Never let them see you sweat (see page 27).

Trinity always stood toe to toe with her partners Neo and Morpheus, and she earned their respect by being the best darn partner they'd ever seen. She was as smart and dedicated as they were and capable of doing the job in a way only a woman could.

Action Heroine Tip #3: When undercover, keep your clothes and your wits about you (see page 101).

When action heroines go deep undercover as everything from a mob wife to a working girl, they must always take pains to look and act the part—and never fail to deliver the goods when it comes time to take down the bad guy.

Action Heroine Tip #4: Be prepared for things to get ugly when it comes time to whack the enemy (see page 136).

I've lured, outwitted, and escaped all types of bad guys—guys with bad bleach jobs and polyester three-piece suits. How did I do it? A pair of handcuffs, the proper footwear, and the occasional bat-of-the-eyelashes-sucker-punch combo.

And Action Heroine Tip #5? That's simple:

Never turn your back on your enemy, never walk away from someone who needs your help, and never get caught without *The Action Heroine's Handbook*.

INTRODUCTION

Greetings, heroines, and congratulations.

You have taken the first step toward becoming an action heroine by realizing a very important fact: *any* woman can become a heroine, including you.

Being an action heroine doesn't come naturally or easily, unless you are an Amazon princess or a vampire slayer (and even they have to endure their fair share of training). Rather, it's about rising to the occasion. Think about it: Ripley didn't set out to rid her spaceship of the mother of all aliens, but she fired up her flamethrower for the good of humanity. Sidney Prescott didn't relish outwitting a knife-wielding psycho, but she wanted to stay alive and kicking. Clarice Starling didn't enter the FBI Academy in order to wine and dine a cannibal, but other seasoned agents somehow didn't savor the assignment.

A heroine's abilities are constantly put to the test without warning, so she must be ready and able to do battle in the all-around competition. This means cross-training in all disciplines, from drinking and dancing to swimming and surfing, using her intuition and instincts to save the world—and looking damned good doing it. With some innate talent and determination, the right training and guidance, and the inherent ability to multi-task, you too can be a first-rate action heroine.

This book is your guide. Within these action-packed pages, you will find everything you need to be a complete action heroine in your own right: tough chick skills, beauty skills, brain skills, brawn skills, and escape skills.

We tracked down real-life heroes and heroines—including FBI agents, sexologists, stuntwomen, beauty queens, drag kings, world-champion boxers, dominatrixes, and detectives—to show us how to develop real-world skills for perilous situations that usually only happen to women with big hair, tight leather pants, and really high heels.

With our step-by-step instructions, you can begin a rigorous training regime immediately. Yoga sessions will aid you in beating a field of laser beams. Years of cheerleading or Tae Kwon Do will give you a wicked kick to bring down a baddie. You can put your talent as a world-class flirt to good use by distracting the enemy with your feminine wiles. (Hint: It's okay to hum the *Wonder Woman* theme song while you do it.)

But take heed: With great ability comes great responsibility. In the wrong hands, the results could be more catastrophic than *Alien: Resurrection*. So after you've learned the skills, keep your handbook under wraps—until a promising apprentice comes along who could benefit from a little heroine training.

Good luck and godspeed, heroines. The world may be looking for a few good men, but it needs many more good action heroines.

CHAPTER 1
Tough Chick Skills

AN ACTION HEROINE might, at first blush, look like an innocent ingénue, a damsel in distress, or a high-maintenance high-heeled diva. But the true heroine welcomes the chance to break a nail or break the rules in the pursuit of justice.

Whooping ass involves more than an unexpected right hook (although that's darn handy). You might need to drink a few thugs under the table to pick up a little cash or keep the peace in your Nepalese outpost. You may need to straddle a hog to escape a band of bikers gone bad. The world is indeed a wacky place, so you need to be fully prepared to ward off a vampire, outwit a Sasquatch, or protect a child from a ferocious beast.

A heroine's toughness might fool a few, but no one will forget that you are 100 percent woman. You can run down perps while strapped into high heels and a bustier. With a body toned by years of yoga, you can stretch and undulate your way through a field of laser beams. You can, if pressed, give birth in rustic conditions…while being pursued by aliens.

You also know that the key to blending in with the boys is to earn their respect. But at the end of the day, it's a whole lot better to be one of the gals—because real women kick butt.

HOW TO WIN A HIGH-SPEED CHASE IN HIGH HEELS AND A BUSTIER

Queen Hippolyte (Cloris Leachman): *Remember, in a world of ordinary mortals, you are a wonder woman.*
—*Wonder Woman*

Unlike male secret agents and superheroes, the action heroine has to do it all—race to the rescue, leap across rooftops, chase down the bad guys—while always looking like a million bucks. And that's where the straps, heels, boning, and lacing come in. Whether you're pounding the pavement or pounding a perp, you have to make it all look easy *and* make sure you don't twist an ankle or jeopardize your bust support. Here's how, according to veteran Hollywood stuntwoman Danielle Burgio.

PREPARATION

- A wide, blocky heel with good ankle support and a closed toe is the best heel for running. Spike heels may look hot, but they are not recommended for jogging, running, or sprinting.
- The bustier should be tight but should not constrict breathing. A tight lacing acts as a brace and will ensure that your breasts will receive maximum support. Lean forward when putting on the bustier, and lace it up the back.

DURING THE CHASE

Step 1: Assume the sprinter's stance.

Pitch slightly over your knees, with your back straight. Bend from the waist so that you're leaning in almost a 45-degree angle. Place your dominant foot forward and under your torso; the other foot should be slightly behind your torso. You should be on the balls of your feet.

Step 2: Push off from the ball of your front foot and hit your stride.

Take long strides and accelerate until you are running as fast as

Keep arms and elbows close to your sides and your body pitched forward.

IT'S ALL ABOUT THE SHOES

Fighting crime is serious business, and the last thing you want to worry about is your footwear. According to podiatrist Dr. Gregory Kaufman, pinched toes, blisters, broken heels, and fallen arches are common for the average Jane, but not for the prepared heroine. With a little foresight—and a spree at the shoe store—you will be ready to kick butt, chase down a villain, or back-flip your way to justice.

- **Motorcycle boots:** These weighty, thick-soled shoes are appropriate for heavy lifting (e.g., a body), low kicking, running through heavily wooded areas, or riding a hog.

- **Thick-soled loafers:** Great for pounding the pavement for long periods of time—whether tailing a good lover gone bad or working undercover as a door-to-door saleswoman (or salesman).

- **Knee-high boots:** Recommended for fencing, horseback riding, and other activities that require support and lower leg protection. Also provide good defense against cuts and bites when trekking in the jungle or heavily forested areas.

- **High-heel boots, pumps:** Ideal for all styles of dancing, with the exception of ballet. An added advantage: They make your backside look perky, so you know you look good coming and going.

- **Ballet slippers:** When stealth and grace are required, ballet flats are the footwear of choice. Tightrope walking, tiptoeing, walking on rooftops, and stretching through laser alarms are just a few heroic pursuits that may employ them.

- **Sneakers:** Perfect for running, jumping, cycling, and kicking. The rubber sole helps you balance if you are standing on something in motion, such as a skateboard, the top of a train, or a person.

- **Stilettos:** Okay for limited ballroom dancing, swaying, and walking. Perfect if you find yourself on a catwalk. Note that the heel itself can be used as a blade. In lieu of a knife or arrow, you can wield your heel—either on the shoe or broken off and used independently—as a piercing instrument.

- **Flip-flops:** Recommended only if you are undercover and trying to look relaxed and casual. They can be removed quickly if you need to jump into barefooted action.

- **Barefoot:** Going shoeless, while lacking in protection of any kind, is best when running on sand, swimming, performing martial arts, and walking on other people's backs.

you can. With arms and elbows pumping close to your sides, remain low to the ground and pitched forward; this will help reduce wind resistance as you sprint.

To help maintain your balance, avoid bringing your knees up as you run. Stay pitched over, with your weight on the balls of your feet.

Step 3: Regulate your breath.
Since your ribs are constricted by a close-fitting bustier, you must take care not to hyperventilate or get easily winded while running. Fight the tendency to take quick, shallow breaths. Instead, be aware of your breathing and take slow, controlled breaths.

Step 4: If the bustier is not giving sufficient support, alter your arm action to restrict breast movement.
Pump your arms straight forward and straight back if your breasts are bouncing side to side. Pump your arms slightly side to side (pushing your elbows slightly outward) if your breasts are bouncing up and down.

Step 5: Create a diversion with your breasts.
If the person you are chasing looks back at you, flash him to distract him or make him stumble.

Step 6: When you catch your quarry, use your shoes as weapons.
Kick your opponent or remove a shoe and use the heel as a club or blade, depending on the heel type. (See "It's All About the Shoes," opposite.)

Virginia Baker (Catherine Zeta-Jones): *Once I get under the first beam, I'm going to be fine. . . . I can do this blindfolded now.*
Mac MacDougal (Sean Connery): *Really?*
        —Entrapment

All of those yoga classes pay off *right now*. Years of conditioning your body with Caterpillar, Downward Dog, Tree Pose, and Sun Salutations give you more than heightened clarity and flexibility; they give you the skill and prowess to maneuver your way through a convoluted web of laser beams. (Not only that—you get to look sexy doing it.) Downward dogging your way through the beams may be slow going, and your muscles will tire; simply remember to breathe and keep your eye on the prize, whether it's that priceless Chinese mask, great gobs of cash, or your masterful con of a master thief. Here's how, according to yoga instructor Nina Vought.

Note: Locate the beams by looking through the viewfinder of a thermal camera or by blowing powder from your compact into the air in front of you (see Appendix A, p. 180). If using the latter method, move through the room to progressively identify the beams, then navigate each laser in turn.

LATERAL MOVES

To step over a laser about 24 inches high, begin from a balanced Tree Pose:

- Center yourself by standing straight with arms at your sides.
- Shift your weight onto one foot and raise your other foot an inch or

two off the floor.

- Use both hands to slowly raise your non-weighted foot to the inside of your opposite leg.

Step 1: From Tree Pose, grab your non-weight bearing big toe.

Grab your big toe with the hand on the same side as the non-weight bearing foot. Stretch your other arm straight out to your side for counterbalance.

Step 2: Straighten your leg directly out in front of you, toward your target, until it is parallel to the ground.

Continue to hold your big toe for balance. Keep your back straight and your foot flexed, with your hips and torso square to your target.

Step 3: Release your big toe and bring your arms back to your sides.

Focus on keeping your leg parallel to the ground and straight out in front of you.

Step 4: Step forward over the laser.

Bring your airborne leg down over the laser, bending at the knee. Touch your toe and then the ball of your foot down onto the floor. Shift your weight forward to that foot by raising your rear foot to the toe and placing your forward foot flat on the floor.

Step 5: Center yourself over your forward foot.

Keep your forward foot planted firmly on the ground. Your rear leg will rise up parallel to the floor. Point your rear foot.

Step 6: Lean forward to form a "T" over your forward foot.

Extend your body from the crown of your head to the tip of your rear toes. Keeping your rear leg, torso, and head in one line, lean down to form a "T" over your forward leg. Extend your arms in front or to the side as needed for balance.

Step 7: Pivot 90 degrees to clear the laser.

With your arms extended for counterbalance, pivot your body 90 degrees on your weight-bearing foot. Turn slowly over your foot and leg.

Step 8: Set your rear leg down.

Raise your torso and lower your leg in line with the other until you are upright.

VERTICAL AND HORIZONTAL MOVES

To slide under a laser as low as 12 inches off the ground and then rise into a standing position, begin from the Caterpillar Pose:

- Get on your knees.
- Sit on the heels of your feet.
- Press your chest into your thighs.
- Point your toes behind you so that the tops of your feet are on the floor.
- Stretch your arms straight out on the floor so that your palms are flat on the surface.

Step 1: Slide your arms forward across the floor and under the laser.

Press your arms so that they slide straight across the floor. Keep your chest and thighs "connected" as long as possible. This will force your torso forward while keeping your rear end high in the air. Keep your chin tucked into your chest.

To stretch under laser beams:

1. Assume the Caterpillar Pose with palms flat.

2. Stretch arms, head, and torso under the beam.

3. Lie flat with hips between lasers.

4. Walk feet toward your hands.

Step 2: Push yourself forward from the knees.

As your chest separates from your thighs, use your knees to propel your hands, arms, head, torso, and hips forward and underneath the laser. Following the path of your hands, move in a wave-like form, pressing your body forward and down to the floor.

Step 3: Move into position for Downward Dog.

Once your hips are flat on the floor and past the laser, flex your feet so that your toes are curled under and pressing on the ground. Keeping your arms hugged into your body, slide your arms back and bend at the elbows so that your hands are flat on the floor directly beneath your shoulders.

Step 4: Raise your hips.

Move your body into the Downward Dog position by tucking your chin into your chest, pressing your hands into the floor, and folding upward at the hips. Your hips will lift to become the highest point on your body. When complete, you will have formed a triangle with the floor (with your hips at the peak).

Step 5: Walk your feet toward your hands.

Slowly inch your feet forward until they are nearly to your hands and continue to fold at the hips. Your legs will be perpendicular to the floor, with your body folded over almost in half.

Step 6: Raise yourself into an upright standing position.

Release the muscles in your neck and tuck your chin to your chest. Keeping your stomach muscles firm, slowly roll into an upright position one vertebrae at a time. Let your arms hang down and follow your torso up. Continue until you are completely upright.

HOW TO POP A NOSE WHEELIE ON A MOTORCYCLE

Spike (Nicky Katt): *You're the chick who won the tunnel run two nights ago.*
Barbara Wilson, aka Batgirl (Alicia Silverstone): *Yeah, that'd be me.*
Spike: *Yeah, well that was kid's stuff. Why don't you take your little tricycle and run along home.*
Barbara: *Why don't we have a side bet?*
        —Batman and Robin

Aside from the delectable sensations of the wind whipping through your hair and having a 1,000-pound hog between your thighs, riding a motorcycle is an indispensable skill when escaping a baddie. Maneuvering through tight spots and turns on a motorcycle, you may be called upon to pop a nose wheelie or stop on a dime to fend off pursuers—or, well, just to impress the heck out of them. They might stop dead in their tracks when they see how high your rear end can get. According to stunt rider Ken Kelley, they're more likely to quit the chase because they're choking on your dust.

A Department of Transportation–approved helmet, leather jacket with back protector, Kevlar gloves, leather riding pants with rear end and knee protectors, and a high pair of thick leather boots are recommended equipment. At the very least, wear a helmet, gloves, and a jacket if your only option is to jump on the bike and go.

PERFORMING THE ROLLING ENDO

A Rolling Endo or nose wheelie—where the rear wheel of your motorcycle comes off the ground and the vehicle continues to roll on its front wheel only—turns the bike into a barrier between you and your pursuers when you are being chased or fired upon from behind. The Rolling Endo requires a large, heavy motorcycle for maximum stability in the roll.

Step 1: Bring the bike to speed.
The ideal speed is about 40 mph.

Step 2: Lean your weight forward to lock up the front shocks.
Position your arms and torso above the front shocks. Press down so that your weight compresses the shocks as far as they can go.

Step 3: Lock the front brake to bring the rear wheel up.
Squeeze the front brake lever on the throttle side of the handlebars so that the front brake locks up. The front wheel will stop spinning and begin to stick, rather than roll, across the surface. The rear end of the bike will begin to rise off the ground.

Step 4: Immediately feather the front brake and find the bike's balance point.
Let off pressure on the front brake to allow the front wheel to once again roll more freely. The more you let off, the more the rear wheel of the bike will fall back down to the surface—and vice versa. Find the balance point on the bike and feather the brake accordingly. Because your weight is now over the front of the bike, the further forward you lean over the handlebars, the further the rear wheel will come off the ground.

Step 5: Adjust your balance to stay on the bike.
Continue to feather the front brake on or off and adjust your weight forward or back. Focus on the balance of the bike to keep steady. Riding a Rolling Endo feels similar to standing on a small skiff that is rocking in every direction.

Lean your weight over the front wheel and squeeze the front brake lever so that the wheel sticks and the back wheel comes off the ground.

Step 6: **When clear of your pursuers, put the rear wheel down.**

Feather off the front brake and shift your weight to the back of the bike to slowly lower the rear wheel back to the surface.

PERFORMING A STOPPIE

A Stoppie—where the rear wheel of your motorcycle comes off the ground and the bike comes to a complete stop on its front wheel only—is useful when racing through alleys or dodging trucks that may pull out in front of you. It will bring the bike to a stop much more quickly than simply applying the brakes. Stoppies are best performed on light motorcycles.

Step 1: Bring the bike to speed.
A Stoppie is dangerous at high speeds, so lower your speed to between 2 and 15 mph before performing the move.

Step 2: Lean your weight forward to lock up the front shocks.
Lean forward from the torso or position yourself above the front shocks so that your weight compresses the shocks as far as they can go.

Step 3: Lock the front brake to bring the rear wheel up.
Squeeze the front brake lever—on the throttle side of the handle-bars—so that the front brake locks up. The rear end of the bike will begin to rise off the ground.

Step 4: Immediately feather the front brake and find the bike's balance point.
Snap the front brake so your back wheel lifts further off the ground, and squeeze the tank with your legs to keep you in the seat. Feather the brake as described in step 4 of "Performing the Rolling Endo" until you can feel it is safe to stop. If you must stop immediately, proceed to step 5.

Step 5: Hold the brake until the bike has stopped.
If you have to stop short, continue to squeeze the front brake. The bike will rear up. To avoid being thrown over the handlebars, let go of the bike and jump off to one side. Push the bike away from you as you jump so that it does not land on you.

Private W. Hudson (Bill Paxton): *Hey Vasquez, have you ever been mistaken
for a man?*
Private J. Vasquez (Jenette Goldstein): *No, have you?*
        —Aliens

Sometimes the world doesn't quite want to accept how truly excep-
tional an action heroine is. Usually, those situations involve a boatload
of testosterone. You may find yourself up against a wee bit of chau-
vinism at work, at the bar, or in a deserted colony on a remote planet.
Longtime protection specialist "Fastball" recommends that you focus
on doing your job well and fitting in rather than standing out. Your
standout status will emerge naturally once you've been accepted into
the fold. Soon enough no one will notice that extra X chromosome
you're carrying around. They'll be too busy asking you to explain
things to them.

Step 1: Talk tough.

Use phrases like "Anytime, anywhere." The tougher you talk, the
more heckling you can fend off. Do not take any trash talk from
anyone in your unit. Use your tough talk to one-up your team, or
be the first one to strike verbally. This may intimidate the others
and stop the trash talk before it starts.

Step 2: Exude a positive, confident, and hard-working attitude.

When there are scheduled exercises or training missions, be the
first one there. Be ready to perform. Even if you are in pain or

otherwise "worked" from the previous day's activities, keep your mouth closed and get straight to work. Do not snivel or complain.

Step 3: Choose a specialty at which you can out-perform the other members of the team.

Focus your development on a specific task that suits your skill set. If you have excellent aim, work twice as hard at your munitions ability. If you are more physically adept, develop your martial arts skills. Do not try to be one of the guys by playing their game— develop an expertise that will enhance your existing skills.

Step 4: Bond with the guys in your unit.

Every special unit has its own code and fraternity. Be a part of this group but do not change who you are to do so. If you are so inclined, join the guys for their outings to bars (see "How to Drink Someone Under the Table," opposite) and strip clubs. Join the group for barbecues or host one yourself.

Step 5: Do not get intimately involved with anyone in your unit.

Everyone in your special unit will be emotionally attached. This makes for a strong, effective, and secure group. You should, however, avoid intimate involvement with a group member at all costs. No matter how much you both intend to keep your physical relationship away from work, the dynamic of the group is bound to be noticeably affected.

Step 6: Be good at what you do.

When push comes to shove, let your work speak for itself. When you excel at what you do, you will gain the respect of the other members in your special unit.

Rachel (Bridget Moynahan): *Hey Lil . . . do we serve water with our whiskey?*
Lil (Maria Bello): *Only water I serve has got barley and hops in it.*
        —*Coyote Ugly*

While an action heroine has absolutely nothing to prove to her male admirers, there's nothing quite like going toe to toe and shot for shot to prove who really wears the pants at the bar. Knowing how to throw back booze can guarantee that you will be the one still standing, be it in a fancy bar or remote Nepalese outpost. The contest ends, of course, when someone gets sick, passes out, or attempts to burn your face with a hot poker. Professional bartender Nick Parkin shows how to keep your wits about you.

BUILDING TOLERANCE

Expect to consume about 10 to 12 shots of hard liquor to successfully drink someone under the table. In order to ingest this much alcohol, you must train to build a high tolerance for its effects. One month before the contest, begin to practice drinking:

- **In addition to your favorite shots, drink a shot of 151 rum every night for one week.**
  If you can typically handle three shots of hard liquor in one night, consume these shots and drink an additional shot of 151 rum every night. Add one shot of hard liquor to your base every subsequent week before the contest.

- **Drink water between the shots.**
  Your body must stay hydrated to keep your liver functioning up to speed.

Step 1: Fill your stomach with a normal-sized meal.
Alcohol is more slowly absorbed into the bloodstream when you have a full stomach. Avoid sushi or Chinese food prior to a drinking contest (see step 2). Eat a typical meal, but do not eat so much that you are overfull.

Step 2: Offer your opponent a meal of sushi or Chinese dishes.
The high proteins in these foods will cause your opponent's metabolism to function faster, causing his body to absorb the alcohol more quickly. His liver, however, will not be able to process a large amount of alcohol at once, so the remaining alcohol will stay in his system and make him feel more drunk more quickly.

Step 3: Prepare your body to process alcohol by consuming one glass of stout beer half an hour to an hour before the competition.
A stout beer is preferable, as it is typically lower in alcohol content (4 to 5 percent) than other beers. The less extraneous alcohol you consume before and during a contest, the better.

Step 4: Focus on the competition.
When you are simply drinking for enjoyment and in a jovial mood, you tend to feel drunk more quickly. Keep a sober demeanor and stay focused on the task at hand. Ignore trash talk from your opponent or any bystanders.

Step 5: Agree upon a straight shot liquor that you both will consume.
Select your favorite liquor for the competition—it will be easier for you to get down.

Use these general guidelines:
- Choose tequila, in 80 to 90 proof. Made from agave—a

cactus-like plant—tequila serves as a stimulant to help you remain alert.

- Choose vodka or whiskey, no more than 80 to 90 proof.
- Stay away from mixed liquor shots (straight liquor plus a liqueur). The sugars in liqueurs will make you feel the effects of the alcohol more quickly.

If you cannot agree on a single liquor, flip a coin.

Step 6: Stay standing throughout the competition.
Stand up before consuming your first shot, and remain standing to help your body burn off some of the alcohol.

Step 7: Drink your shots without affect.
Both you and your opponent should drink at the same time. Take your shot and knock it back. Do not contort your face. Stare your opponent directly in the eyes and drink your shot as if it were water.

Step 8: When it appears that your opponent is nearly incapacitated, order a harder shot.
The gauges of drunkenness in order of appearance are euphoria, excitement, confusion, stupor, coma, and death.

When your opponent exhibits excitement or confusion, order a combination shot with any two liquors. Gauge your own level of inebriation and be certain that you have the tolerance to consume the shot before ordering.

Step 9: Consume the shot and claim victory.
When your opponent collapses, cannot finish the shot, or vomits, you have successfully put him under the table.

Drew (Chris Toloa): *You really think you can surf it for real out there?*
Anne Marie (Kate Bosworth): *Well, Drew, I dated you, I guess I can do anything.*
　　　—*Blue Crush*

The pipe: an awesome tube-like wave of water that looks even more impressive with a surfer hanging 10 through its green walls. That's where you come in. Whether you're an undercover agent trying to bring a band of surfing bank robbers to justice or you're out to prove you can surf with the big boys at a major competition, you need to know how to ride out the mother of all waves. This stunt is recommended for advanced heroines only, by Surfing Hall of Famers Kathy Jo Anderson and Lisa Wakely Muir.

Step 1: Enter the water with your board under your arm.

Attach the board to your leg via the safety strap only if there are many other surfers present. (An unsecured board is easier for you to handle, but poses a hazard to other surfers nearby if you wipe out.) Walk into the water until it is between knee and waist high. As you enter, note whether the waves are breaking to the left or to the right.

Step 2: Lie flat on your board and paddle to the area where the waves begin to crash and turn up whitecaps.

With your head toward the front of the board (and away from shore), lie belly-down on the board. Use a "crawl" stroke with your arms to paddle out beyond the break of the waves.

Step 3: Move straight through the waves as you come to them.

To avoid being rolled by the waves, stay perpendicular to them. If you have a shorter board, "duck dive" under the wave by pressing the nose of your board under the wave as it passes. The water will pass between your body and your board.

If you have a longer board, "turtle" it by rolling a 360-degree turn underwater, with the fin side of the board facing up as the wave passes. Continue your 360-degree roll so that you are above the water after the wave has cleared.

Step 4: Turn the board so that it faces the shore.

Step 5: Catch a wave at its crest.

Paddle so that your speed matches the speed of a wave and you meet it just before it begins to break. If you are too far in front of the wave, it will break on top of you and cause you to wipe out. If you are too far behind the wave, you may miss it.

Step 6: Quickly stand up on your board and turn it away from the break.

As the wave begins to take your board, stand up so that your front foot is toward the center and your back foot is toward the rear of the board. Extend your arms out to your sides for balance. Bend your knees slightly in a balanced athletic position. Swing the nose of the board to the right or left by turning your shoulders and body

WIPEOUTS AND OTHER DANGERS

- Do not touch—or let your board touch—the impact zone of a barreling wave. The impact zone is where the top of the wave breaks and meets the bottom of the wave. This may snap your board.

- When you wipe out, wrap your arms over your head with your elbows tucked around your ears and curl your body into a ball. You will be the thrown by the wave, so ride it out. Let the wave take you, but continue to protect your head from impact with the ocean floor or your own board.

To surf a barreling wave:

1. Paddle to meet the wave at its crest.

2. Stand on your board and turn away from the break.

3. Drag your hand in the water to back into the tube.

4. Lower your rear end toward the board to fit in the tube.

in the direction you want to go. Turn your board away from the crest and look sideways down the wave.

Step 7: Surf on the face of the wave.
Once you're centered on the wave, keep a consistent line.

Step 8: Listen for a barreling of the wave.
If you are riding a steep wave (with off-shore winds) and you hear a hollow echoing behind you, the wave's break may be forming a full, hollow tube or barreling wave—also known as a "green room" or "glass house."

Step 9: Drag your hand in the water to "back into" the tube.
Slow yourself by trailing the hand closest to the face of the wave in the water. This will allow the tube to catch up with you, essentially "backing" your board into the tube.

Step 10: Tuck to conform to the size of the tube.
Barreling waves may create tubes of 3 to 15 feet in diameter. Lower your rear end toward the board by bending at the waist and knees so that you fit in the tube. Keep your upper arms to your sides, extending your hands and lower arms for balance.

Step 11: Ride the wave inside the tube until it tapers off or closes.
If the wave gets smaller or tapers off, just ride it out. Lower yourself back onto your belly on your board as the wave subsides. If the wave does not get smaller, slow yourself down by dragging the hand closest to the face of the wave in the water (as above) until the wave collapses over you. This will cause a wipeout but may be the best exit if the barrel is large.

HOW TO RESCUE
A DROWNING SWIMMER

C. J. Parker (Pamela Anderson): *I can't imagine doing anything else. My mom said I was born with a red rescue can in my hands.*
        —Baywatch

The most important beach skill is not choosing the right swimsuit or applying sunscreen evenly. Though these skills can certainly come in handy, the sun-loving heroine's most important talent is her knowledge of the ocean rescue. But the most effective lifeguards don't run across the beach in skimpy suits for nothing. Use the run to call attention to your save—grab two wide-eyed gawkers and put them to use. And follow these instructions from lifeguard trainer Linda Delzeit-McIntyre.

BEFORE YOU MAKE THE SAVE

Making an ocean save in particularly harrowing conditions—high winds, storms, or heavy swells or currents—could be more dangerous than heroic. Proceed with the following steps only after you've determined that:

- Emergency teams are too far off to save the victim.
- You are strong and skilled enough to swim the distance to the victim and drag him back to safety.

Step 1: Spot the victim in the ocean.
The up and down swell of the ocean may cause him to temporarily disappear from sight. Keep your eyes on a fixed line between yourself and the struggling swimmer. This will be your target line.

Step 2: Designate another person to call paramedics, then notify emergency lifeguard teams in the area.

Lifeguards practice their rescue plans routinely, but they may not be readily available. While another person calls, you can focus on making the rescue.

Step 3: Secure back-up assistance from those around you.

Ask two of the nearest people who appear mature and responsible to assist you. Have one of them help you locate equipment (see step 4), while the other watches the victim and confirms the target line. The latter person will also keep a close eye on you if and when you and your other assistant enter the water.

Step 4: Locate and use common items found on the beach to assist you in making the save:

- Swim fins to help you reach the victim once you're in the water and help you return to the beach faster.
- Surfboard or boogie board to aid in flotation.
- A section of rope or dog leash 4 to 6 feet in length, and one or two intact 1-gallon plastic bottles with tight lids. Use a double square knot to tie the empty bottle(s) to one end of the rope for the victim to use as a flotation device.

MAKING THE SAVE

Ideally, you will enter the water with another swimmer while your other assistant watches both of you, as well as the victim, from shore. As you swim to the victim, your backup swimmer should follow you out with a surfboard or larger flotation device.

Use a sidestroke to swim the victim to safety.

Step 1: Remove your shoes, secure your equipment, and run across the beach on your target line.

Tuck any flotation devices under your arm. If you are using swim fins, do not put them on until you have reached the water. Bare feet are much more effective when running across sand.

Step 2: Run into the water on your target line and begin swimming.

When the water reaches waist level, dive in and begin swimming toward your target along the bottom of the ocean. Use dolphin-style kicks and grab the sand to help propel you forward. If you cannot see the victim when you come up for air, have your assistant direct you to the victim's last known location.

Step 3: Pace yourself to conserve energy.

Swim to the victim as quickly as you can while retaining at least

50 percent of your energy. You'll need to have energy to swim back with the victim. If you feel that your breathing is labored or that your muscles are tiring, slow your pace.

Step 4: Once you are within your flotation device's reach of the victim, toss it to him.
Secure one end of the rope or leash to your arm or waist using a slipknot that can easily be removed if the victim panics and attempts to pull you down, then throw the flotation device to the victim.

Step 5: Calm the victim before proceeding back to shore.
Be sure that the victim has a firm hold on the flotation device. Speak in clear and simple language to calm and direct the victim.

Step 6: Swim the victim to safety.
Use a sidestroke to swim to safety. Look back at the victim frequently to make sure he is still secured to the flotation device. If a boat is nearby, swim the victim toward it; otherwise, swim to shore.

Step 7: Provide first aid if necessary.
Wrap the victim in a towel or blanket to keep him warm and treat shock. Stretch his legs and arms to treat cramped muscles. Get the victim breathing in through the nose and out through the mouth to treat his anxiety. Turn the victim on his side if he vomits—this will clear any ingested water and open his airway.

Step 8: Warm yourself after the victim is secure.
Wrap yourself in a blanket or towel to prevent shock or hypothermia.

Buffy (Sarah Michelle Gellar): *Oh, come on. A stake through the heart, a little sunlight. . . . It's like falling off a log.*
—*Buffy the Vampire Slayer*

An action heroine must be prepared to face anyone and anything, including an insurgent from the grave. Garlic, crucifixes, and holy water are actually tried-and-true weapons for warding off the undead, according to the Right Reverend Sean Manchester. Add speed and an ability to swim to your arsenal, and you'll soon be stopping vampires and zombies dead in their tracks. Just to be safe, light a few incense sticks when you get home. In this case, there's no such thing as overkill.

Note: One of the most difficult problems when it comes to fending off the undead is determining who is truly undead and who is simply unwell or involved in an elaborate fantasy or delusion. Accurate identification is your best defense (see chart on p. 42).

FENDING OFF THE UNDEAD

As the undead by nature have many supernatural abilities—extra strength, extra speed, and so forth—it is best to avoid physical confrontation and combat at all costs.

Step 1: Present a cross or crucifix to their line of sight.

The undead generally turn from the sight of a cross. If a crucifix is not available, place one stick perpendicular to a slightly longer stick to form a cross.

HOW TO RECOGNIZE THE UNDEAD

Attributes The undead may be:	Etiology	Alternate causation
Pale and lean.	The bodies of the undead do not decompose after burial but generally maintain a lean appearance when not feeding. An undead body that is not sated on blood will also appear exceedingly pale.	Lack of sunlight due to heavy undergraduate studies; participation in Gothic culture; disciple of Atkins diet.
Puffed and bloated.	Bodies of the undead expand after feeding.	Glandular condition.
Full lipped, to shield sharp teeth.	Indicates a vampiric condition, usually the result of a bite inflicted by another member of the undead.	Collagen or Botox treatment; chipped or broken teeth.
Foul smelling.	Though technically not fully decomposing, the body will typically retain the smell of death.	General poor personal hygiene and grooming.
Trickling blood near the corners of the mouth or wearing stained clothing.	Evidence of a recent blood feeding.	Messy pasta technique (note, however, that tomato sauce is typically lighter in color than blood).
Staring severely for extended periods of time.	The undead do not need to regularly refresh and cleanse the cornea.	Individual under the influence of a controlled substance.

Step 2: Splash the undead with holy water.

Holy water burns the undead in the same way a viscous acid might burn the living. Other clear liquids (vodka, rubbing alcohol) will generally not serve the same purpose, although they will sting the eyes when applied.

Step 3: Burn incense.

Frankincense can be found at any incense retailer. Light a stick to protect a specific room or area. Alternatively, wave a stick in front of the purportedly undead individual.

Step 4: Adorn yourself with herbs.

The undead are allergic to whitehorn, buckhorn, and garlic. Purchase these at a local herb shop and carry them with you at all times. Use sparingly.

Step 5: Run.

Once you have completed steps 1 through 4 to slow or stun your undead predator, protect your neck with your shoulders, collar, or scarf and move away from the undead as quickly as possible.

Step 6: Find a river with fast running water.

The undead cannot enter running water—they must use a bridge or shallow opening to cross. Swim to the other side of the river and continue your escape. If there is a bridge nearby that your undead pursuer can cross, swim downstream in the middle of the river to continue your getaway.

Anthropologist: *Bigfoot's not playing games anymore.*
  —Night of the Demon

Sasquatch, Bigfoot, Yeti. A beast by any other name still smells. Although sighted worldwide, Sasquatch (derived from the Coast Salish Indian term for "monkey-man") seem to favor the backwoods of North America. In the United States alone, they have been spotted approximately 1,500 times. Listen closely for signs that a Bigfoot is afoot and vacate the area with super-speed when you spot one. Here is your Sasquatch primer, from Bigfoot Research Organization curator Richard Noll.

Step 1: Determine whether you are in Bigfoot territory.
  Sasquatch thrive in heavily forested areas in climates with considerable precipitation, away from human traffic, with water,

---

BIGFOOT FACTS

- Bigfoots measure as much as 10 feet tall and weigh between 500 and 1,200 pounds.

- Bigfoots may be provoked by aggressive domestic dogs of any size.

- Bigfoots have distinctive five-toed footprints—up to 20 inches long and 7 inches wide—with a very long stride.

- Bigfoots sometimes emit a sickening odor, described by witnesses as a cross between a dead animal and a wet dog.

- Bigfoots may mimic other animal noises as a form of lure.

Create a distraction by throwing a stick away from the Sasquatch, toward the forest.

game, fish, and vegetation readily available. Areas hospitable to Bigfoot exist all over the world, but you are most likely to encounter one on a forest service or fire road at dawn or dusk.

Step 2: Listen.

If a Bigfoot senses your presence, it may take cover behind a tree or large bush or freeze in place. Keep your ears open for cracking branches, heavy bipedal footfalls, rustling groundcover, or unfamiliar grunts, howls, or hoots.

Step 3: When you spot a Bigfoot—or when it spots you—do not make prolonged eye contact.

Most sightings have been at a comfortable distance beyond 50 feet. Looking down may be interpreted as a sign of submission, and thus may incline the Bigfoot to tolerate your presence. Keep the Sasquatch in your peripheral vision.

Step 4: Do not show your teeth.

Baring your teeth may be interpreted as an act of aggression.

Step 5: Fool the Sasquatch into thinking you are another creature of the forest.

A Sasquatch will usually keep itself far enough away to observe you unnoticed. If, however, you're in close proximity, mimic the Bigfoot's current behavior—kneel down, eat berries or vegetation—to signal that you are not a threat.

Step 6: Cause a distraction.

Bigfoots are about as intelligent as the great apes (gorillas, chimpanzees, orangutans) in that they do not use fire or tools and are easily distracted. Throw a rock or stick into the forest to create a loud noise and draw the Bigfoot's attention away from you. DO NOT throw anything *at* the Bigfoot.

Step 7: Evacuate the area as quickly and as calmly as possible.

Once you are out of its sight, you can be reasonably certain that you are no longer in danger.

Special Agent Dana Scully (Gillian Anderson)*: This is my baby! Please don't let them take it.*
        —The X Files

Action heroines are used to getting themselves out of a lot of tight spots, but they may some day find themselves faced with a little action hero or heroine who wants to get out of a tight spot, too. The best action heroines never let physical complications get in the way of protecting the innocent, investigating wood chippers, or even eluding aliens—and giving birth is no exception. According to Nan H. Troiano, RN, MSN, with the aid of a trusted ally, you can safely bear down and birth your baby. (You don't, however, have to grin and bear it.)

PREPARATION

Step 1: Collect the following supplies:
- Two new or very clean shoelaces
- Clean scissors (if in doubt, soak in alcohol, hold over a flame, and then wipe away the carbon film, or drop in boiling water for 5 to 10 minutes)
- Two small blankets (warmed if possible)
- A cap for the baby's head (a large sock or clean, warmed cloth will also work)
- A tarp, drop cloth, or large blanket

Step 2: Remove external stressors.
    Find a quiet space, dim the lights, put on calming music, light a

candle to focus on during the birth, light a fire or turn up the heat, and ask a calm, level-headed person to assist you. Ignore any external distractions, be it gunfire, aliens, or flowing magma.

LABOR

Step 1: Assume the position.
If you think delivery of your baby is imminent—you will feel an overwhelming urge to "bear down" or push—sit in a chair or on the floor against the wall. Position your back at about a 45-degree angle against the chair back or wall. Put a blanket, tarp, or drop cloth under you to catch any blood or fluid discharged. Take off your pants or skirt, and drape a cloth over your pelvic area.

Step 2: Take slow, deep breaths in through your nose and out through your mouth.
If you start to hyperventilate, breathe slowly into a small paper bag or while cupping your hands over your mouth and nose. You should feel better in a matter of minutes.

Step 3: Listen to your body and push down.
While timing contractions can provide clues to when it is time to give birth, they can be misleading, especially if you are delivering early. When it is time to push, you will know it. At this point, push or "bear down." You will usually need to push for about 10 seconds two to three times during each contraction.

Step 4: Relax, breathe slowly, and rest between contractions.
Continue to take slow, deep breaths through your nose and exhale through your mouth.

2 small blankets

2 shoelaces

Clean scissors

Baby's cap

Candles for focus

Drop cloth

Take slow, deep breaths in through the nose and out through the mouth.

DELIVERY

Step 1: Deliver the head of the baby.

The crown of the baby's head will most likely be the first to emerge. After the head is out of the birth canal, instruct your assistant to check around the neck for the umbilical cord. If the cord is wrapped around the baby's neck, the assistant should slip a finger between the cord and the baby. She should loosen it and attempt to slip it around the baby's head. If it is too tight, direct her to tie off the umbilical cord (see step 5).

Step 2: Deliver the head and shoulders.

The next couple of contractions will usually cause you to push/bear down and deliver the shoulders and body of the baby. The baby will be very slippery. A large gush of fluid usually comes out of the birth canal at the same time. Have your assistant crouch low to the ground, close to the birth canal, to catch the baby as she emerges. Your assistant's hands should be as wide apart as possible, palms up, and close to the birth canal.

Step 3: Widen the birth canal.

If several contractions pass and, despite your best pushing, the shoulders do not come out, pull your knees back toward your chest during a contraction and push. This will widen the birth canal. The rest of the baby should appear in short order.

Step 4: Have your assistant hold the baby as the placenta is expelled.

Once the baby is out of you, your assistant should not pull on the umbilical cord. The placenta will usually separate from the uterus and follow the baby out within minutes. Have your assistant save the placenta in a plastic bag to be analyzed by a doctor later.

Step 5: Tie off the umbilical cord.

Instruct your assistant to hold the baby level with—never higher than—the birth canal. She should use the shoelaces to make two tight knots two inches apart on the umbilical cord, then cut the cord between the two knots with clean scissors.

Step 6: Clean and dry the baby's mouth and nose.

Do this immediately, before she makes her first cry. If the baby is not breathing, vigorously dry her arms, legs, and abdomen with a dry blanket. Flick her heels with your middle finger and thumb. The baby should start kicking and crying.

Step 7: Warm the baby.

Wrap her in a clean blanket. Put a hat or large clean sock on her head. You can also put the naked baby against your skin and pull a blanket over both of you.

Step 8: Check for uterine bleeding.

The average blood loss during childbirth is 250 to 500 ccs, or the equivalent of 1 to 2 large cups of coffee. (More than 500 ccs of blood loss could indicate hemorrhaging.) If you continue to bleed after the placenta has been removed, start breastfeeding. This will help the uterus to contract. You or your assistant should also rub slow, firm circles over the uterus—this is the area around and below the belly button. The uterus should feel like a small, firm grapefruit. If it feels soft and spongy, continue massaging the area until the uterus contracts and firms up.

Step 9: As soon as you are able, seek medical attention for you and your baby.

HOW TO PROTECT YOUR CHILD FROM A FEROCIOUS BEAST

Ripley (Sigourney Weaver): *Get away from her, you bitch!*
    —Aliens

There's nothing quite like a cute kid in distress to bring out the protective badass in you. Whether a child is being threatened by a rabid dog or a freakish alien beast, you must take immediate action. Allow your latent maternal instinct or even your "pick on someone your own size" mentality to kick in. Russ Smith of the Los Angeles Zoo recommends that you create a distraction, place yourself between the beauty and the beast, and get the child to safety. When it's all over, sit her down and give her a few tips on protecting herself. It's never too early to train the next generation of action heroines.

Step 1: Draw the beast's attention onto you.
Call, yell, or throw an object toward the beast so that it knows you are present.

Step 2: Make yourself and your child appear as large as you can.
From a standing position, raise your arms above you or out to your sides. Direct your child to do the same. This will indicate that you are not a meal but rather a force to be reckoned with.

Step 3: Stand your ground.
Do *not* step toward the beast. This may be interpreted as an act of aggression and may cause the beast to rush at you before you are prepared to act. Instead, stand fast to show the beast that you are not intimidated by it.

AVOIDING CONFRONTATION

The best way to protect your child from a potentially vicious creature is to teach her how to safely avoid a confrontation in the first place.

- **She should not pull on a potentially vicious creature's tail or otherwise engage it in aggressive confrontation.**

- **She should not approach the creature while it is eating. It will instinctively defend its food by attacking anyone or anything appearing to threaten it.**

- **When confronted by the creature, she should hold very still and maintain eye contact. The creature will be attracted to movement and may mistake a sprinting child (or parent) for a meal.**

Step 4: Slowly move yourself between the beast and your child.

Do not have your child move toward you. (Her smallness will make her a more appealing target.) When you reach your child, place her directly behind you. The beast may understand that your only purpose is to protect your child, and may back away. If it decides to rush you instead, proceed to step 5.

Step 5: Get your child to safety by quickly raising her to a safe position at least 10 feet off the ground.

This will allow you to focus your energies on outwitting the beast rather than on protecting your child.

Step 6: As the beast continues toward you, look for any object large enough to serve as an obstacle between you and it.

Choose an object—tree, wall, and so forth—that will both slow down the creature's forward momentum and limit its ability to get to you from above. Be sure to keep your eyes on the beast. If it steps around the object to the left, you should continue around the other side. Perform the same move if the beast steps around to the right.

Wield a sharp
defensive object.

Keep your eyes
on the beast at all times.

Place yourself
between the beast
and the child.

Raise your arms out to your sides and direct the child
to do the same to appear as large as possible.

CONFRONTATION DON'TS

Never purposefully approach the creature.
Always give it the right of way.

Do not run.
The creature may have the ability to move very quickly—as fast as or faster than humans—for very short distances.

Do not attempt to swim away.
The creature may be a good swimmer and could catch up to you in the water.

Step 7: Find a long, pointed defensive object.

Use a stiff, forked branch from a tree, a pitchfork, or similar object native to your surroundings.

Step 8: Fend off the beast.

Sharply push the beast away by jabbing or shoving your weapon into the beast's side or neck.

Alternatively, attack the beast from behind: Use both hands to grab the creature at the point where his neck attaches to his skull. Use a half- or full-Nelson hold. Run both of your arms under the creature's armpits and up so that your hands lock behind its neck. Maintain this hold until the beast is incapacitated. Take care to avoid any tail action, which may deliver a hefty blow.

Step 9: Remove yourself and your child from the area.

Keep yourself between the beast and your child, and direct your child to move from the area to safety. Move slowly and deliberately, never turning your back on the creature, so you can track its movements.

CHAPTER 2
Beauty Skills

AN ACTION HEROINE will do whatever it takes to get her man, even if it means having to use her feminine wiles. If turning a man into a sex pawn will help you gain access to a villain's lair, it will be well worth the sacrifice.

Remember, however, that even Wonder Woman wasn't born a ready-made bombshell. As Diana Prince, she had to doff her glasses, let down her raven locks, and trade in her sensible work suits for a sultry superhero costume. With only a few essentials, a restroom, and a few spare minutes, you too can turn yourself into a hottie, whether it's to distract the enemy or seduce a Greaser with a heart of gold.

In the world of action heroines, you may find yourself forced to pose as a stripper to plant a bug or dance like a maniac and shake things up at the local ballet academy. You even may be called upon to tango with the enemy. (P.S. It's okay to enjoy it.)

But be warned: It's not all fun and glam. You might expect scrapes, broken bones, and bruises as you go about saving the world, but you also need to be prepared for the more mundane pains of plucking, waxing, exfoliating, polishing, and bleaching. When you finally nab your man, the price of beauty will be worth the effort.

Danny (John Travolta): ***SANDY!!!!!!***
Sandy (Olivia Newton-John): ***Tell me about it, stud.***
     —Grease

Whether you need to transform yourself on the fly to seduce a mysterious agent or you have to make yourself over fast to fit in with the in-crowd, it's critical for the action heroine to have a few fashion tricks up her sleeve. *Cosmopolitan* beauty director Rachel Hayes recommends tucking a small emergency kit into your handbag to guarantee that you'll be turning heads while you're turning the tables on your target. Assess your surroundings and improvise with items you may have around you. All's fair in love, war, and looking hot.

Your emergency kit should include: lipstick; mascara; bronzer; shimmer stick or shimmer powder; bobby pins; hair elastics; fast-drying, light-colored nail polish; scissors; clear packing tape; mirror; hand lotion; hair gel; velcro rollers; hairspray; buffing cloth or chamois.

Step 1: Head to a public restroom.

Rip off a portion of a fresh, unused toilet seat covering to blot perspiration or shininess. It is made of virtually the same material as blotting paper.

Step 2: Apply a deep or vivid lipstick to focus attention on your mouth.

Swipe on a red lipstick to look sexy or elegant, a deep burgundy to look vampy, or a shiny lip gloss to ratchet up the sex factor. Lipstick can also double as blush in a pinch. If you are lacking a mirror when applying lipstick, you can use a shiny knife, window, chrome bumper, or other reflective surface to check out your reflection. If you don't have any lipstick, rub a dry paper towel across your lips for a temporary flush. Bite your lips as necessary throughout the evening to re-redden them.

Step 3: Apply several coats of mascara.

Allow each coat to dry before reapplying. Separate lashes with a small brush or comb after each coat.

Step 4: Change your hairstyle.

If you have a defined or narrow face, slick back your hair with water. Pat hair gel or a small amount of hand lotion on your hair to set the style. If your hair is long, put it up in a messy ponytail or twist. For action heroine volume, divide your hair into a few different sections, roll hair into large Velcro rollers (toilet paper rolls can be used in a pinch), spritz with hairspray, and blast your head with a hair dryer or stick it under the hand dryer in the restroom.

Step 5: Bust out your cleavage.

You can give a boost to your bust by adding bronzer to your cleavage. Use a darker bronzer in the V of your chest to define your cleavage and a lighter shimmer powder or stick to the tops of your breasts. For serious cleavage, tape up your breasts with duct tape or clear packing tape. Start under one arm and unroll the tape under the breasts in a straight line beneath the other arm.

Once your cleavage has been plumped up, show it off. Unbutton one or more buttons on your blouse, shed any extra layers you may be wearing, turn around a sweater if the back is lower than the front, or unbutton a shirt completely and wrap it around your body, tucking the ends into your waistband.

Before | After

Apply makeup, add volume to your hair, and emphasize your cleavage.

Step 6: Add sparkle.

Any sheer or shimmery product can be used to highlight the neck, collarbone, jawline, cheekbones, legs, shoulders, or any area to which you want to draw attention.

Step 7: Tend to your fingernails and toes.

Apply lotion or even a touch of olive oil to the cuticles and nails to smooth out rough skin and make your nails look shiny. If you want color, use a fast-drying polish. Buff your fingernails with a cloth if you don't have time to apply nail polish.

Step 8: Exit the restroom and dazzle your target.

Do not look around to see who is watching you—*know* that everyone is. Walk with confidence and ooze sensuality.

Nomi Malone (Elizabeth Berkley): *I'm not a whore, I'm a dancer!*
         —Showgirls

Every action heroine worth her salt has a lot of skills in her arsenal. In addition to running, jumping, shooting, kicking, and all those run-of-the-mill talents, a real heroine knows the value of mastering a few key dance moves. Since you never know when you're going to be called into duty to tango with the enemy, shock the crowd at a summer resort or dance club, or bare all in the name of truth, justice, and the action heroine way, it pays to be prepared. With a killer pair of stilettos and a whole lot of moxie, you can take on the world, one dance floor at a time. Here's how, according to dancer/choreographer Cynthia Fleming and stripper Shannon Cromwell.

HOW TO TANGO

Step 1: Look the part.

Dancing the tango requires a dramatic ensemble. Wear a slinky dress with a deep slit and neckline. Wear a padded bra. Slick back your hair and pin a flower over one ear. Wear heels as high as possible but also as comfortable as possible for dancing. If you are dancing in front of a large group of people, apply more eye and lip makeup than you would normally wear. Do not look at your partner while dancing; it will add to the drama.

Step 2: Assume the basic position.

Your partner will lead and maneuver you around the dance floor. Lift your chest as if you are a confident matador. Place your left hand over his right arm and against his right shoulder blade. Place your right hand in his left hand. Your elbows should be lifted and out to your sides. You are now in "close hold."

Step 3: Master the basic step.
The tango is a 5-count dance: slow, slow, quick, quick, slow. Starting on your right foot, take three long steps backward on the balls of your feet (right, left, right and slow, slow, quick). The remaining two counts involve one fluid step. Quickly step out to the side with your left foot and slide your right foot over to join it.

Step 4: Improvise.
The tango is a dance of passion and pursuit. You can be as dramatic as you dare.

- In time to the music, wrap your leg around your partner's waist on the fourth count and let him drag you across the floor for the next five counts.
- Allow your partner to dip you. As he bends you back, extend your left leg in the air on the fourth and fifth counts.
- Turn your back on your partner on the first count, wrap your arms back around him, and grab hold of his buttocks. Turn back into your partner on the fourth count.
- Circle each other for all five counts as if you are stalking prey, keeping your chest lifted. Stay on the balls of your feet and resume close hold on the last count.
- Break position with your partner and trail one arm from your head down over your body, while you dance the basic step or any tango combination.
- Walk purposefully in a passé step, bringing each leg up and rubbing it against the other leg as you raise and lower it to the floor. All movements should have purpose and be in time to the music.

To own the dance floor:

Assume the basic tango position.

Allow your partner to dip you and extend your leg.

To dance like a maniac, run in place and whip your head around.

To striptease, assume a persona and remove clothes very slowly.

When attempting the "Flashdance" look, it's important not to wear shoes; wrap up your feet with athletic tape instead and add leg warmers and ripped sweatshirts for effect. Wear your hair in an untamed mane.

Step 1: Drench yourself in water, then head to the dance floor.
When you first hit the dance floor, run in place, rub your hands in circles over your thighs, and shake your head from side to side. Other dancers will move away to avoid your spray, giving you space to bust a move. Ask friends to throw drinks at you to keep you drenched.

Step 2: Avoid eye contact.
This dance is all about you, so keep your focus inward.

Step 3: Punch it up.
Punch the air in front of you and kick your legs out in turn as you skip in a circle.

Step 4: Do some floorwork.
With your back to the floor, use your arms to support your upper body and position your body in a straight plank position. Bend your right leg slightly and cross it over your left leg until your right foot is completely on the ground. Shift your weight to your right leg and repeat with the other leg. You are rhythm now.

Step 5: Roll your head.
When you are tired of working the floor, stand up and work in a new move. With your arms out to your sides, roll your head down

and back repeatedly while turning your body around in a circle. Let your hair whip around you wildly.

HOW TO STRIPTEASE

Step 1: Develop a character.
The sexy librarian is an evergreen favorite. You could also be a teacher, cowgirl, business executive, nurse, flight attendant, or any other job where the clothing is distinctive and can be layered.

Step 2: Layer garments appropriate to your character.
Start with lingerie, such as seamed stockings, garter belts, and lacy bras. Add shirts, skirts, and sweaters that you can unbutton or unzip. Avoid anything that has to be pulled over your head.

Step 3: Wear high heels.
The added height will make your butt look high and round.

Step 4: Accessorize.
Put your hair up or under a hat so you can let it down during your striptease. Wear glasses. Carry a ruler if you prefer to go as a teacher; use it to discipline a naughty "student."

Step 5: Select a song for your strip that appeals to you.
It can be slow and emotional or fast-paced and frenetic, but the more you connect with it, the more you can emphasize your moves.

Step 6: As you begin your dance, start to connect with your audience.
Rub your hands over areas where your audience would like to put

their hands. Make eye contact with members of your audience and undress them with your eyes.

Step 7: Pace your strip so that you continue to undress throughout the song.
Tease by unbuttoning your clothes very, very slowly. Take breaks from undressing to bend over and look back at your audience between your legs. If you have props, such as a pole, a 4-poster bed, whipped cream, or a riding crop, creatively incorporate them into your dance. Flash some cleavage, thigh, or butt.

Step 8: Tantalize your admirers.
Whisper sexy things in an audience member's ear and exhale softly on his neck. Let him feel your heat and softness, but only for a moment. Run your loose hair over his face. Powder yourself with a puff to stay cool and dry; the feminine smell will drive those who get close to you wild. For an audience of one, turn your back to him and sit on his lap. Slide down between his legs and look back at him.

Step 9: Continue dancing until you have nothing more to remove, or the music ends.
Make your exit with attitude.

Pola (Marilyn Monroe): *Do you know who I'd like to marry?*
Loco (Betty Grable): *Who?*
Pola: *Rockefeller.*
Loco: *Which one?*
Pola: *I don't care.*
　　　　—How to Marry a Millionaire

A millionaire's cash might keep him warm at night, but can a thick portfolio accompany him to the opera or drive his sportscar like it corners on rails? Of course not. He's looking for a woman with model looks and a Mensa mind. He wants a fit, stylish woman who is at an age to bear an heir. What he wants is an action heroine just like you—he just doesn't know it yet. Millionaire's Club CEO Patti Stanger provides tips on baiting your hook.

IDENTIFY YOUR QUARRY

You can identify a millionaire by his material trappings—where he lives, the places he frequents, the car he drives, and how he dresses.

Use the following techniques to track your millionaire:

- Attend polo matches.
- Check out luxury cars at dealerships.
- Take sailing lessons or lunch at the yacht club.
- Have a drink at the bar or around the fireplace of a swank resort.
- Shop and ask questions at electronic stores, particularly near the large-screen televisions.
- Have a drink in the clubhouse at a country club.
- Take tennis lessons at an exclusive gym.

HOOK YOUR MILLIONAIRE

Step 1: Step out on the town . . . alone.

Visit the bar at upscale hotels and restaurants, Mondays through Thursdays from 5 to 7 P.M.

Step 2: Locate and make eye contact with a wealthy-looking man.

While millionaires come in all shapes and sizes, they will without fail all sport an expensive watch from Rolex, Cartier, Breitling, or Tag Heuer. The high-profile millionaire will be impeccably dressed, well-coiffed, in shape, and at all the right parties. The low-profile millionaire could probably use a haircut and need to lose five pounds. (It's best to check out his wrist for an expensive timepiece before passing judgment based on his appearance.)

When you do catch his eye, smile and hold his gaze for five seconds. Wait for him to approach you before speaking.

Step 3: Check that he is not wearing a wedding ring and does not have a visible tan line where a ring would normally be.

Well-coiffed hair

Top-shelf liquor

Trim physique

Expensive watch

No wedding ring

Fine cigar

Expensive loafers

The high-profile millionaire can be found at the bar of upscale hotels and restaurants.

Getting involved with a married man will not lead to a satisfying relationship and goes beyond the call of action heroine duty.

Step 4: Allow him to buy your second and subsequent drinks.

Sip slowly and demurely. Do not get drunk.

Step 5: Talk to him.

Do not discuss money. Let him lead the conversation and look for common interests that you can discuss.

Step 6: Carefully convey your interest.

Your body language should express interest and grace. Never cross your arms across your chest. Stand up straight; a classic "first position" ballerina's pose is very elegant.

Step 7: Remain open to physical contact, but do not make the first move.

Do not try to be overly sexy, and do not touch him first.

Step 8: Let him pay the bill.

When the bill arrives, thank him for a lovely evening.

Step 9: Remain open to a subsequent date, but do not initiate it.

Show interest, but do not make yourself available if he asks you out at the last minute.

Step 10: Take things slowly.

Do not sleep with your millionaire on your first date or early in your relationship. Make sure that you have him hooked and that he's not seeing anyone else before you decide to take things to a more intimate level.

Mike Swale (Peter Berg): *I'm starting to feel like a . . .*
Bridget Gregory (Linda Fiorentino): *Sex object?*
　　—The Last Seduction

Whether you have to reclaim your riches from your ex or simply take cover in a stranger's apartment, it helps to have someone else ready, willing, and able to do your dirty work. The professional dominatrixes at Philadelphia's Olde English Chambers reveal that a little stroking, ego or otherwise, will usually do the trick, but it's sometimes necessary to unleash your inner vixen to whip a man into submission. (Just don't have too much fun—remember, you're on the job.)

Step 1: Play it cool.

Once you have keyed in on a potential sex pawn, catch his eye, then quickly look away and appear disinterested. If he attempts to get your attention, respond with only slight interest. Smile at his jokes; do not laugh at them. If he touches your arm, allow him to leave his hand where it is but do not reciprocate the contact.

Step 2: Make him prove his worth.

Make it clear that he has to come up with something that is valuable or useful to you to earn a place in your life or bed. If he's a trainer at a gym, he can help you maximize your workouts. If he's a chef, he can cook for you. If he's in finance, he can assist you in investing. He will believe that you are becoming dependent on him (when, of course, it's really the other way around).

Step 3: Find his erogenous zone.

While talking to him in public or private, touch his ears, forearm, neck, cheek, fingers, and chest. If he draws in his breath sharply or moans, you have found his spot. Stroking or casually rubbing this spot will excite your mark. He will crave your touch.

Step 4: Offer him something unique to make him further dependent on you.

Offer a special sexual technique or position he can experience only with you. Dole out your unique talent infrequently. It will keep your sex pawn off guard and always asking for more.

Step 5: Judge your subject's response to your requests.

If he responds favorably to strict orders, further enslave him by becoming more demanding. Ask him to pick you up from work, pick up your dry cleaning, buy groceries, take your pet to the vet, change your oil, or any other menial task you can think of. Occasionally exchange a sexual favor for a task.

Step 6: Make him work hard to please you.

Hide your pleasure during sex: In fact, yawn. Act as if you do not care to see him more than occasionally. Cancel dates at the last minute, find excuses not to see him, and wait to respond to e-mails. You will hold the power in the relationship.

Step 7: Use him to your advantage.

Demand that he do your bidding, whether it's offing a bad guy, destroying incriminating evidence, or taking a bullet for you. He is conditioned to want to please you, and will not resist your demands.

HOW TO SEDUCE THE ENEMY

Matty Walker (Kathleen Turner) to Ned Racine (William Hurt): *You're not too smart, are you? I like that in a man.*
            —Body Heat

After a long, hard day of chasing down bad guys, most action hero-ines crave nothing more than a long soak in the tub. But the action heroine's days—and nights—never end. You may never need to go so far as sleeping with the enemy, but you might very well be called in to play footsie with a felon or dupe an evildoer over drinks, to access his wallet, plant a bug in his bedroom, or distract him long enough to thwart his plans to rule the world. Sexologist Carol Queen shares her seduction secrets here.

Step 1: Dress to accentuate your best physical assets.
Wear anything that makes you feel sexy (see "Clothing Guaran-teed to Distract the Enemy," p. 75). A catsuit will show off your curves, a bikini will show off your skin, and a loose, flowing gar-ment can reveal something unexpected, such as a flash of skin or black lace bra.

Step 2: Position yourself in his line of vision.
Make sure you take the room's lighting into account—you want to be attractively lit but always visible, so sitting closer to him is better than sitting far away. Look at him with purpose and confi-dence. He will feel your eyes on him.

Step 3: Catch the enemy's eye.
Let your eyes linger on your target. Hold his gaze to convey your strength and intent. Your attention will pique his interest.

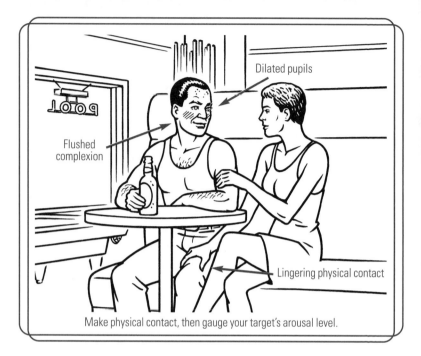

Dilated pupils

Flushed complexion

Lingering physical contact

Make physical contact, then gauge your target's arousal level.

Step 4: Give good conversation.

If he does not start up a conversation within a short period of time, approach him. Saying "Come here often?" is cliché but laden with suggestion, so do not be afraid to use it. Alternatively, start a conversation about something substantive, then steer the discussion in a more personal/intimate/erotic direction. Erotic banter laced with double entendres will further convey your desire.

Step 5: Make physical contact.

Rub up to or bump into him "accidentally" and linger over the contact. Gently hold his chin to look in his eyes. Grab his wrist to check the time. Simply touch his forearm or thigh to emphasize a point.

CLOTHING GUARANTEED TO DISTRACT THE ENEMY

There are some tried and true items any action heroine should have stocked in her closet. When combined with a confident attitude, these garments, undergarments, and accessories are guaranteed to turn a few heads and turn the tables on your enemy.

▪ High heels.
An obvious action heroine staple, high heels of all sorts are sexy. A pointy toe and pointy heel are especially sexy. An open-toe shoe with a great pedicure is sexy. Mid-calf boots are sexy. (Make sure the shaft of the boot is fitted to your leg. It should not encase your calf like a sausage, but your leg should not rattle around in the boot, either.)

▪ A quality push-up or demi-cup bra.
Insert silicone "cutlets" if you need a boost, usually under and to the sides of your breasts. If you are small-chested, go braless. Unbutton an extra button on your blouse so that your bra or cleavage peeks through.

▪ A great pair of sunglasses.
The bigger the better. The enemy will not have any idea of what you are thinking or what you are looking at with your eyes obscured by dark lenses.

▪ Sensual fabrics and textures.
A cashmere sweater, a silk charmeuse blouse, leather pants, anything in lycra, and fishnet stockings are all alluring additions to an outfit. Mixing up textures, such as fur with sheer, will catch the eye of both friend and foe.

▪ Clothes that wrap.
Surprise your target with an unexpected flash of skin: Reveal a deep slit in your wrap skirt or take off a jacket (one shoulder at a time) to expose a halter top and a bare back.

▪ A touch of menswear.
A men's white oxford or baseball cap, when paired with well-cut jeans with frayed hems and a rhinestone belt, can knock a man off his feet.

▪ Well-placed jewelry.
Wear a necklace that draws the eye to your cleavage, earrings that swing and reflect off the neck, an arm band or wrist cuff to draw the eye to a well-sculpted bicep or your strong hands. Lace jewelry, such as a choker or wide bracelet, can fool your opponent into thinking you are demure and innocent.

Step 6: Gauge his reaction.

Your target will be giving off signals, whether he's interested or not. He may be looking away in an effort to resist your charms. He may be staring into your eyes to build sexual energy. A change in breathing, dilated pupils, or flushed complexion indicate a high level of arousal.

Step 7: Wait for him to make the first move.

If he's doing any of the following, you have him on the hook:

- Finding excuses to touch you
- Saying or whispering sexy things
- Buying you drinks
- Leaning in and closing the distance between you
- Making lingering eye contact
- Looking at your lips when you speak

Step 8: If verbal sparring or calculated touching do not prompt your target to make the first move, take the initiative yourself.

By this point, objective analysis and intuition should indicate whether your seduction attempts are working. If he is not engaged in your conversation, is not looking at you or making much eye contact, does not seem appreciative of your attractiveness, is checking his watch, looks or sounds distracted, and refrains from touching you, you need to initiate contact. Run your hands over his chest, take his face in your hands and move in for a kiss, or verbally proposition him. Say something like, "I feel the energy between us is too strong to resist." You will know immediately if your seduction is a success.

Step 9: Retire to a more private setting to continue the seduction.

Suggest that you go back to his place or hotel room, where you can both get more comfortable.

Step 10: Once you have completed your seduction, leave at once.

Gather your things—making sure to leave nothing behind—and make your escape. Conceal any items you have lifted from him, be it a key, notebook, or security card. It is best to vanish while he is in the shower, on the phone, or momentarily distracted. Note that he will be left wanting more, so do not be surprised if he tries to locate you (see "How to Fake Your Own Death," p. 148).

CHAPTER 3
Brain Skills

IN ADDITION TO to invisible planes, slinky catsuits, and man-crushing thighs, an action heroine also has to possess mental agility, be it to read lips to track a conversation without the aid of a bionic ear or to endure a lengthy interrogation without the aid of underwear. Moxie and a level head will get you far and, more importantly, keep you safe when outwitting a band of burglars in your brownstone, facing off with a silverback gorilla in the jungle, or profiling a serial killer with the help of a crazy cannibal.

If you happen to be a double agent or costumed super-hero, be prepared to juggle one or more secret identities in your ongoing pursuit of justice: To bring down a bitter pageant coordinator, you may have to go undercover as a beauty contestant. To infiltrate a men's club, poker game, or restroom, you may have to pose as a man, replete with bulge. To rifle a mafioso's wallet, you just may have to take on the role of "working girl."

In this chapter, you'll learn how to use your brainpower to keep your cover, keep your cool, and most of all, keep yourself alive.

Clarice Starling (Jodie Foster): *Most serial killers keep some sort of trophies from their victims.*
Hannibal Lecter (Anthony Hopkins): *I didn't.*
Clarice: *No. . . . You ate yours.*
> —*Silence of the Lambs*

Action heroines who cross paths with a serial killer need to know the basics of profiling. Profiling allows you to evaluate clues to determine whether you are indeed dealing with a psychopath or just some wanna-be copycat. According to forensic psychologist John Dicke and security expert Shawn Engbrecht, true psychopaths typically have no conscience but possess a keen intelligence. But then again, your instincts and intellect are nothing to sneeze at, either. As soon as you identify the offender, report your findings to the authorities. Then go home, put your feet up, and enjoy a nice glass of Chianti.

Step 1: Research his childhood.

A serial killer is usually a white male between 20 and 40 who had a traumatic childhood. He may have suffered abuse from or been abandoned by a parent, usually his mother. He may have been adopted or lived in a foster home. As a child, the suspect may have wet the bed at an age older than usual, started fires, and shown cruelty to small animals—particularly cats.

Track down his earlier residences. Present yourself as an old friend and talk to his former landlord or family members. A call to the county clerk can also uncover public records, such as divorce and family court documents. If you can determine where he attended school, interview former teachers about his early behavior and academic performance.

Step 2: Analyze his work history and "stick-to-it-iveness."

A serial killer lacks follow-through in most areas of his life, including his education. He will have a lousy job history and a spotty attendance record.

Posing as an employer checking references, contact the suspect's former place(s) of employment and ask for information regarding work performance and attendance as well as verified academic degrees and diplomas.

Step 3: Look for signs of a dissociative personality.

A serial killer may only remember his crimes as a spectator or in a dreamlike, dissociative state. When checking out his work history and interviewing coworkers or neighbors, look for evidence that he's forgetful, loses track of time, and shows up late or not at all for work or other appointments.

Step 4: Observe his social life.

A serial killer is likely to be a loner. He will have inadequate relationships with women. If he is married or has a girlfriend, he will have a superficial relationship and perceive intimacy as a threat. He may show little interest in his partner sexually, masturbate, read copious porn, and frequent peep shows and strip joints.

With a partner, stake out the suspect at his job, near his residence, and in any establishment he frequents. Befriend the woman in his life and casually extract information.

Step 5: Study his modus operandi.

The method of murder for most serial killers becomes a ritual of sorts; they will often pick up their victims—usually women—in the same location and kill them in a similar manner. In order to preserve the memory of a murder, the killer will often take some sort of memento from the victim, be it a body part, lock of hair, or item of clothing. These items may be on his person or in a designated "trophy" area. Do not attempt to search for trophies unless you are certain the suspect is nowhere in the area.

Step 6: Stake out the scene of the crime.

Serial killers often like to return to crime scenes or gravesites in order to relive the experience. Attend a victim's funeral and look for anyone suspicious lurking in the crowd or at a distance. Stake out the crime scene on significant anniversaries of the murder.

Step 7: Wait for the suspect to slip up.

Like a drug addict or alcoholic, a serial killer will have a progressively greater need for a "hit" and may kill more frequently and frantically. Because of this compulsive drive and feelings of grandiosity, he will take more risks and be more likely to slip up because he thinks he cannot be caught. By tailing your suspect, you may catch him in a minor infraction that could uncover more serious evidence. Partner with one or several people to stake him out around the clock. He can be tripped up on something as minor as a parking ticket or because neighbors have complained that his apartment smells bad.

Step 8: Report your evidence to the authorities.

Once your suspect slips up and you have sufficient evidence, based on his patterns and behavior, that your suspect is a killer (and a repeat offender at that), report your findings to the authorities so he can be brought to justice.

HOW TO EAVESDROP FROM A DISTANCE

Frances Stevens (Grace Kelly) to John "The Cat" Robie (Cary Grant): *From where I sat it looked as though you were conjugating some irregular verbs.*
—*To Catch a Thief*

To stay one step ahead of your enemies, you must know their every move. Without the help of a well-equipped, battery-powered ear canal—or a multi-processor, hydraulically enhanced canine partner— you must develop the ability to "hear" with your eyes. With killer eyesight, binoculars, and a clear line of vision, you can learn to decipher any conversation, provided you know the language in which your target is mouthing off. Speech and language pathologist Linda Kessler says that reading lips requires a lot of practice. (Try honing your skills on that catty broad across the courtyard who's always talking behind your back.)

Speech reading a conversation requires a significant amount of preparation. Familiarize yourself with the following procedures before you have to put them to use.

Step 1: Determine the topic of conversation beforehand.

Knowing the topic will help "limit" the vocabulary used in conversation. Read up on the subject matter, whether it is banal or unusual. Pay close attention to the vocabulary used—this will help you key in to complicated words as they are spoken.

Step 2: Position yourself in front of or to the side of the speaker.

Position yourself in front of the speaker to see lip movements and vowels more clearly. Position yourself to one side of the speaker to see tongue movements more clearly. Your position is a matter of personal preference and which movements you're more adept at reading. If necessary, use a combination of positions to help understand the conversation. (See step 4.)

Step 3: Position yourself within a reasonable proximity to the speaker.

If your vision is fair, you may be able to read a conversation across a moderately sized room—for example, at a party or restaurant. If your vision is not as strong and closer proximity is not an option—for example, at the opera or on a distant street corner—obtain a line-of-sight on the conversation with a pair of binoculars or a zoom lens.

Step 4: Stay mobile.

You may need to adjust your location to read a conversation. A speaker may turn or shift from side to side, causing you to miss key points. Keep on your toes and adapt to the situation as needed.

Step 5: Read the conversation using the following basic criteria.

Use the following principles to read consonant sounds:

- *P*, *B*, and *M* are formed with both lips together.
- *F* and *V* are formed with the top teeth on the bottom lip.
- *Sh*, *Ch*, *J*, *Y*, and *Zh* are formed with the lips in a large pucker.
- *Th* is formed with the tip of the tongue sticking out between the upper and lower teeth.
- *S (C)* and *Z (X)* are formed by the lips making a smile.
- *R* is formed by the lips making a small pucker.
- *W* is formed by the lips making a closed pucker.
- *K* (hard *C*, *Q*), *G* (hard), and *H* are formed with an open (neutral) mouth and are never perceptible. Experience and context will help you discern the consonant.

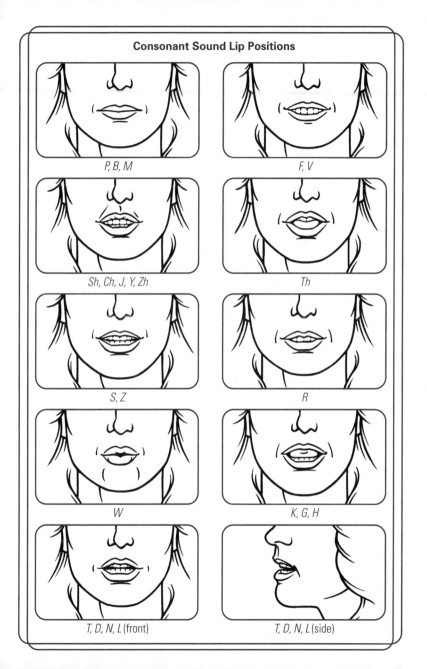

Consonant Sound Lip Positions

P, B, M

F, V

Sh, Ch, J, Y, Zh

Th

S, Z

R

W

K, G, H

T, D, N, L (front)

T, D, N, L (side)

- *T*, *D*, *N*, and *L* are formed with the tip of the tongue moving up to the top of the mouth and then down (seldom perceptible). A side view position will better allow you to view tongue movement.

Step 6: Determine the vowel sounds through context.

Vowel sounds are formed by both the shape and the degree of opening of the lips. Each vowel has a unique look. For example, a smiling mouth, slightly open, will form the "i" in "mit"; when slightly less open it will form the "ee" in "meet." Determining vowel sounds is more complicated than reading consonants, since the variations and combinations are much more numerous and vary in performance. Attempt to read vowels through context, as you glean the consonant sounds.

Step 7: Mentally combine the shapes seen on the speaker's lips to follow the words in the sentence.

Sometimes the ability to follow the sentence only happens after the sentence is completed—and then things just click. The better you can see the lips, and the more angles you can see the speaker from, the more likely you will be able to read lips successfully.

Do not get stuck on one difficult word. Words that are difficult to read (one with several sounds you can't see, a proper noun, an unusual word, a long word, or words beginning with a vowel sound) can sometimes be understood within the context of the words surrounding them.

HOW TO INVESTIGATE YOUR SPOUSE/LOVER

Emily (Gwyneth Paltrow): *That's not happiness to see me, is it?*
        —A Perfect Murder

While love can be a many-splendored thing, it can also leave you vulnerable and confused. Trust your instincts—if something feels wrong, it usually is. Gather and look at the facts. If your man has nothing serious to hide, breathe a sigh of relief. But if he isn't being straight with you and is trying to murder you for your trust fund, get out of the relationship immediately. Fight the temptation to go medieval on his ass. Don't worry; he'll get his in the end. The information here comes from Date Smart investigator Carmen Naimish.

Step 1: Prepare to go undercover.

Purchase a wig with a style and color significantly different from your own hair as well as a pair of large-rim glasses with clear or tinted lenses. Rent or borrow a vehicle from a friend to avoid using your own. Gather bottled water, food, a notepad and several writing instruments, binoculars, recording devices (camera and/or video camera), and cell phones or walkie-talkies for you and a second investigator (if possible) to use for communication. Do not bring reading material.

Step 2: Watch his place of business.

In disguise, drive to his place of business in the middle of his workday—be there before or after lunch, when he is more likely to be leaving or arriving. Drive through the parking area to look for his vehicle in the parking lot. The company may have assigned parking—if he has a set spot, locate the exit closest to his car that will allow you to tail him or make a quick getaway should the need arise (see "Setting Up a Stakeout," p. 90).

Step 3: Watch other locations he frequents.

Use the same surveillance techniques for other locations he told you he often visits. Pay particular attention to his health club and favorite bar: These are common places to leave en route to a tryst. If he is not where he said he would be, you may assume that he is lying to you.

Step 4: Enlist a second investigator when tailing your spouse.

Follow your spouse for only a short distance, staying at least one or two car lengths back when driving in traffic, and then pass him off—via mobile phone or walkie-talkie—to a second investigator. He or she should follow your spouse and keep in close communication with you to set up the next "pass off" location. Use this leapfrog technique until your spouse arrives at his destination.

WHEN TO BE SUSPICIOUS

It is a good idea to investigate your spouse or lover if any of the following conditions are met:

- **He seems "too good to be true."**

- **He claims he is in the CIA or can't tell you exactly what he does for a living.**

- **He is elusive about his past.**

- **He asks for money or use of your credit cards.**

- **He claims that he has little or no family.**

- **His routine changes unexpectedly or his behavior becomes more aggressive.**

Locate a spot where you can observe his office building door and his vehicle, then use binoculars or a zoom lens to get a closer look.

SETTING UP A STAKEOUT

Whether you're setting up surveillance at your spouse's workplace or another location, set yourself up in a spot from which you can observe both the door of the
building as well as his vehicle.

- **Park your vehicle so that you will have a quick, unobstructed way out. Use street corners or park just in front of or behind fire hydrants. Do not park in loading zones.**

- **Avoid parking in bank lots—this is a sure way to arouse suspicion and attention from the police.**

- **Move your vehicle frequently when parked in a residential area. Unfamiliar cars sitting for extended periods may arouse the suspicion of the neighbors and police.**

- **Use binoculars or the zoom lens on a camera to get a closer look at your spouse.**

- **Use writing instruments and paper or a voice recorder to make notes of times, dates, places, and your spouse's activities.**

Step 5: Determine whether your husband is being truthful with you.

Compare the data you gathered through surveillance to see if his
story holds water. If things add up, stick with him. If there are too
many holes in his story, confront him.

Step 6: Keep you and your loved ones out of danger.

If you are concerned for your safety and simply want to leave
(see "How to Maintain a Secret Identity," p. 112), do so; alert
the authorities once you've reached a safe location. If you have
children or other family members in the area and need to protect
them, confront your spouse in a public place or with several
friends present. If your life or security is in jeopardy, do not
confront him at all; just leave.

HOW TO SURVIVE AS A MOB WIFE

Karen Hill (Lorraine Bracco): *I know there are women like my best friends who would have gotten out of there the minute their boyfriend gave them a gun to hide. But I didn't. I gotta admit the truth. It turned me on.*
—Goodfellas

The key to being a mob wife is to never let on how much you know or how smart you really are. Don't play dumb exactly; rather, just stay in the background and soak up information. Quietly study the law, tax codes, and insurance policies. Quietly sock money away. Quietly go about the business of raising your kids in as normal an environment as is possible when all of your furniture apparently "fell off a truck." And if your husband ever goes down, quietly move on. This guide is provided by veteran cop and mob connoisseur Rick Porrello.

Step 1: Do not ask your husband too many questions.
Knowing too much about your husband's business might come back to haunt you. If he is charged with a crime but you do not know where he was at the time, you may not be considered an accessory (but be prepared to be called on to give testimony).

Step 2: Become familiar with state and federal law.
Visit a law library or otherwise research state and federal laws regarding organized crime. Use the knowledge to insulate yourself and your children from prosecution.

Step 3: Socialize your children outside the "family."
Whether your husband gets pinched or the entire family joins the witness protection program, your children will be better off having lived as normal a life as possible. Send them to camp, sign

them up for sports teams, and encourage them to participate in activities outside the "family."

Step 4: Encourage your college-age children to study law and/or medicine.
Having a doctor or a lawyer in the family may be helpful if your husband gets arrested or takes a bullet in the backside.

Step 5: Take out a life insurance policy on your husband.
It may be difficult for him to qualify for insurance unless his cover is particularly thorough, but in your husband's line of work, the threat of sudden death is far too high to be uninsured. If your husband disappears, determine your state's term limit for declaring missing persons dead so that you can redeem the policy.

Step 6: Pay off your assets and put them in your name.
If moveable assets—car, home, and so forth—are in your name, they may (depending on your husband's charges) be more difficult for the IRS or other governmental agencies to confiscate. If your husband is charged with a tax-related crime, you can use these assets to pay for his legal defense. If he gets whacked, you'll have the assets to cover your most immediate needs. (Be aware, however, that if your husband is convicted of racketeering and organized crime, it may not make a difference whose name the assets are in.)

Step 7: Establish a plan for a secondary income.
If your husband is arrested, you may need to take on extra work. Consider writing a mob-related novel or cookbook or auctioning your high-profile mobster's clothes, jewelry, or autographed mug shots.

Step 8: Enjoy the good life while you can.
Nothing lasts forever, especially in the world of organized crime.

HOW TO KEEP YOUR COOL UNDER INTERROGATION

John Correli (Wayne Knight): *There's no smoking in this building, Ms. Tramell.*
Catherine Tramell (Sharon Stone): *What're you going to do? Charge me with smoking?*
    —*Basic Instinct*

Even an action heroine can get a bit of grief now and again. People sometimes want to assume the worst of you, but you know the truth. You were home, sleeping alone, when that rock star's career was brought to an early end by someone whose hair, fingerprints, and car match your own. When the cops come to haul you in, stay calm and trust that justice—and a timely shift in your seat—will ultimately prevail. Detective Chip Morgan provides just the facts for proclaiming your innocence.

Step 1: When the authorities arrive, determine why you are being questioned.
If you are simply being questioned at the scene of a crime or at your home or business and aren't required to go anywhere, cooperate with the authorities as best you can.

If you are asked to go to the police station, find out if your cooperation is mandatory. If you are forced to go to another location for questioning (e.g., the police station), you are under arrest (whether or not those exact words are explicitly stated), and you have the right to call an attorney. Do so.

Step 2: Change your clothes before voluntarily leaving with the police.
Before you go with the authorities, slip into something more comfortable—if you feel comfortable in your clothes, you will be more relaxed. (Underwear is optional.) If you aren't allowed to change your clothing, then you are in custody. Ask for your attorney.

Step 3: Exude confidence on the ride to the station and throughout the interview.

Do not be cocky or bitchy, but appear unaffected by the interrogator's questions or innuendo. Be polite and courteous.

Step 4: Answer questions clearly and concisely.

Think briefly about your answer before responding to a question. If you can answer "yes" or "no," do so, but don't be trapped into yes or no answers if the question requires a more thorough explanation. Explain as much as necessary and answer in truthful and nonevasive terms. Say, "No, I didn't do that" rather than "Do I look like the kind of person who would do that?"

Step 5: Request that very general questions be clarified.

Keep the interviewer's questions focused on the event at hand. If you are being questioned about your past, ask the interviewer what your past has to do with the current incident. As in step 3, do not be aggressive. If you are innocent, you have every right to question the authorities who are questioning you.

Step 6: Use positive nonverbal communication.

Interviewers look for "tells" or nonverbal cues (sweating, shifting your eyes or position in a chair) that might indicate you are lying. Look your interviewer directly in the eye when you answer a question, but do not stare him down. Staring might be misinterpreted as a challenge to his authority. Sit up straight in your chair and directly face your interviewer. Let your arms fall naturally to your sides, rest your hands on your thighs, and keep both feet flat on the floor. Don't slouch, look away, sit sideways to the interviewer, or cross your arms or legs. These may all be interpreted as signs of deception or defensiveness.

Confident demeanor

Direct gaze

Erect posture

Comfortable clothing

Feet flat on floor

Sit up straight, rest your hands on your thighs, and look your interviewer in the eyes.

AVOIDING A FALSE-POSITIVE POLYGRAPH

Savvy action heroines—especially those being framed—must know how to avoid a "false-positive" polygraph result (when a truthful person reacts strongly during the test and is mistakenly deemed deceptive).

- **Insist on a "single-issue" test in which the examiner questions you about only one incident. The human body responds (with raised pulse, blood pressure, etc.) to the issue that presents the most immediate threat. If you are being questioned about a shooting as well as running a red light, your responses to questions on the less serious incident may read as strongly as those questions on the shooting. If more than one issue needs to be resolved, suggest that you will submit to several separate tests.**

- **Tell the truth to the best of your knowledge, as you understand it.**

- **Don't worry about being nervous. Nervousness does not register in the same manner as deception.**

- **Do not attempt countermeasures. Stepping on a tack or thinking of a stressful situation when asked a simple question is a surefire way to fail a test. If the examiner uncovers your measures, he will deem you to be deceptive.**

Step 7: Proclaim your innocence with emotion, but not endlessly.

Interrogators are taught that only guilty people will sit without anger through a prolonged interview while they are being accused of committing a crime. Forcefully state that you are innocent and repeat this if necessary. When you've had enough, it's okay to tell your interviewer that you are finished talking.

Step 8: Offer to take a polygraph to prove your innocence.

Most law enforcement entities (cops, prosecutors, and even judges) trust modern polygraph results. Even if they don't ultimately schedule you for an examination, the mere fact that you offered to take a polygraph is an indicator of truthfulness.

HOW TO OUTWIT A BAND OF HOME INTRUDERS

Lydia (Ann Magnuson): *You're a woman, you're living alone now. Your alarm goes off, or you hear glass break, or for whatever reason you think someone's broken into your home in the middle of the night. What are you going to do? Call the police and wait until they get here on Tuesday? Traipse downstairs in your sexy little underthings and check it out? I think not!*
—*Panic Room*

As the queen of the castle, you must defend your home against all types of marauders—from termites to burglars. Put fortifications in place long before you are called upon to rid your home of criminals. Security veteran Chris McGoey recommends battening down the hatches, installing alarm systems, and practicing commonsense security measures. You may not be able to purchase a panic room, but you can be savvy enough not to buy into fear. You already possess the greatest safeguard of all: your wily intellect. In the face of your cunning, home intruders don't stand a chance.

PREPARATION

Step 1: Secure points of entry.

Use solid wood or metal doors with heavy-duty deadbolt locks and strike plates with three-inch screws. Always lock windows securely and use secondary blocking devices like wooden dowels.

Step 2: Practice regular home safety.

- Use a peephole to determine who is at your door.
- Use infrared motion sensor lights outdoors.

SAFE ROOM CONFIGURATION

Create a room where you may easily hide and access outside help if necessary.

- Select a closet or interior room. The room's only entry should be a door—no window, skylight, or chimney access.

- Install a solid core wood or steel door with a peephole and a steel door jam. The door should open outward so that it cannot be kicked in.

- Supply the room with necessary items—a cell phone with charger, a flashlight, a first-aid kit, water, and weapons (gun, pepper spray, baseball bat, or hockey stick). If you can, wire an access panel for your home's alarm system into this room to limit burglars' access to the alarm controls.

- Activate your alarm system whenever you retire for the night.
- Call the police and notify neighbors to report any suspicious activities.

Step 3: Create a plan before your home is invaded.

Examine the potential points of entry and establish an escape route for each entry scenario. If you have the means, establish a "safe room" that you can quickly access in case of home invasion.

WHEN A BREAK-IN OCCURS

Take steps to avoid confrontation and get to safety.

Step 1: Attempt to exit the house.

If you or a member of your family can get out, do so. Use windows, doors, or the roof to exit immediately. Jump through a window or off a balcony if this is your only means of survival. Use fire ladders, trees, or bushes to escape from upper levels. Once you are out of the house, call the authorities. If you are unable to escape, proceed to step 2.

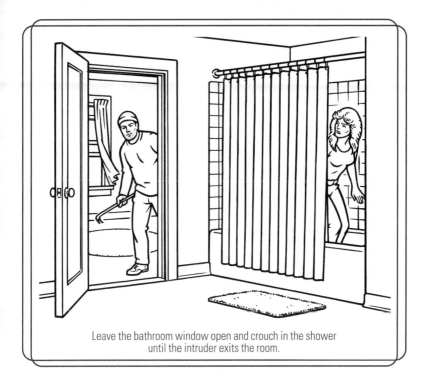

Leave the bathroom window open and crouch in the shower
until the intruder exits the room.

Note: If you are on any life-sustaining medications—insulin, nitro-glycerin, etc.—take them with you before you exit your home.

Step 2: If you have a safe room, get to it as soon as possible.
Lock yourselves in and contact the authorities. Do not exit the safe room until the authorities have arrived and controlled the situation. Be sure to view their identification—passed under the door—before exiting the safe room.

Step 3: If you cannot escape, attempt to call the authorities by any means necessary.
Program your telephones' speed dial or voice dial to automatically

---

ESCAPE FROM A BATHROOM

If you are being chased, try to escape through a bathroom.

- **Enter the bathroom. Close, lock, and barricade the door, and open the window.**

- **If the window will allow you a safe exit, jump out and run as quickly as you can to safety.**

- **If you do not have enough time to escape through the window, leave the window open and hide in a cabinet under the sink or in the shower with the curtains drawn. Chances are the intruder will assume you made it through the window. Once he leaves the room, make your exit safely out the window.**

---

call the police at the touch of a button or utterance of the word "help." (Alternatively, if you cannot get through, call a family member and have them make the call to the authorities.) Give the dispatcher your name and address and tell her that there are intruders in the house. Say your lives are in immediate danger and that the intruders have guns. Leave the phone off the hook or activate a speakerphone option so that the authorities may listen.

Step 4: Activate your alarm system panic mode.

The activated system will gain the attention of your alarm monitoring company and neighbors.

Step 5: If confronted by the intruders, keep a cool head.

Attempt to cooperate with the intruders as long as it doesn't involve harm to you or your family.

Step 6: Fight only as a last option.

If you have the means, the training, or the opportunity to fight back, and your lives are at stake, do so with all your might. Use two fingers to deliver an eye gouge or a throat jab to the notch at the base of the intruder's neck. Disable your opponents, then run.

HOW TO GO UNDERCOVER

Gracie Hart (Sandra Bullock): *I'm in a dress, I have gel in my hair, I haven't slept all night, I'm starved, and I'm armed! Don't mess with me!*
  —*Miss Congeniality*

Action heroines can truly do it all. They can also be it all. In order to bring down baddies, you may have to pose as a prostitute, a beauty contestant, or even, gulp, a man. With creative costuming, a plausible backstory, and a generous supply of tape, you can assume your cover role with ease. To suspend your colleagues' disbelief, you'll need to eat and breathe your cover 24-7, even if that means repeatedly professing your desire for world peace, getting groped by prospective Johns, or adjusting your "bulge." The wealth of information comes from former Philadelphia cop Dennis Spillman, beauty queen Kate Wilson, working girl "Pleasure," and drag king Jo-El Schult.

UNDERCOVER BASICS

The essentials of undercover work are the same no matter what your cover. To prepare, use the following guidelines.

- **Scope out your surroundings.** Identify escape routes as well as poorly lit or dangerous areas.
- **Blend into your surroundings.** Above all, avoid looking like a cop, special agent, or action heroine.
- **Make up a believable backstory.** Pull from your own life experiences. For instance, if your mother was an actual beauty queen, mention that you entered this beauty pageant to follow in her footsteps.
- **Place yourself in proximity to your suspect.** An opportunity will present itself when you can witness something going down.
- **Engage a suspect in small talk**. Once he seems comfortable and

easy talking with you, steer him toward a line of discussion that will yield incriminating information or clues.

To blend in with the ultimate glamazons—the beauty queens—you'll have to buff, bake, tape, spray, oil, and wax yourself into pageant-perfect condition. The hardest part might be concealing your weapon during the swimsuit competition. Remember to smile, smile, smile; you will draw all eyes up and away from any unsightly bulges.

TO PREPARE FOR THE PAGEANT

Step 1: Obtain appropriate credentials.

Most pageants have age requirements. If you have "aged out" of competition, acquire an age-appropriate birth certificate to meet the age eligibility. You will need to supply a copy of your birth certificate at all levels of competition.

While you do not need to supply proof, you will have to sign a contract stipulating that you have never been married or pregnant.

Step 2: Prepare your pageant-perfect look.

Devote yourself to tanning prior to the competition. Wax key areas of your body (mustaches, armpits, and bikini lines). Amp up your workouts prior to the competition and put yourself on a protein-rich, low-carb diet.

Step 3: Cultivate a passable talent.

Do's:

- Singing (old standards—"Orange-Colored Sky," "O Mio

Bambino Caro," or "Art Is Calling for Me"—or any number from the musical *Jekyll & Hyde*)

- Tap dancing
- Jazz dancing
- Ballet
- Baton twirling
- Playing flute
- Playing violin
- Playing piano

Don'ts:

- Performing an unusual talent (it will only draw attention to your lack of pageant experience)
- Singing Top 40, pop, and rap songs
- Playing French horn
- Playing drums
- Playing clarinet

Step 4: Pack an emergency kit.

Carry a handbag with any and all of the following items: bobby pins, waterproof mascara, false eyelashes, lipstick, lip gloss, mirror, Firm Grip, duct tape, hair spray, nude-colored stockings and knee-high stockings, and any other makeup you plan to wear. Leave enough room in your handbag to conceal your weapon, cell phone, listening device, or other gear (see Appendix A, p. 180).

AT THE PAGEANT

Step 1: Blend in with the other contestants.

Do not drink. Do not smoke. Do not do drugs. Do not swear. Do not talk about sex. Do not discuss your eating disorder. Others in the pageant *will* report you, and your chaperone will be stuck to you like glue throughout the entire pageant. Make contact with your handler or coworkers on the outside while you are drawing a bath or preparing to shower in a locked bathroom.

Step 2: Maintain your appearance.

Makeup and hair should be "done" at all times. Add false eyelashes and a bright-colored lipstick before going onstage. Hair, which can be long or short, should have volume and bounce and cover any earpiece you are wearing.

Step 3: Enhance your cleavage for the swimsuit and evening gown competitions.

Tape up your breasts during the competition using duct tape or clear packing tape. Start under one arm and stretch the tape under the breasts in a straight line to the same position under the other arm. This will push breasts up and together to create cleavage and allow you to conceal a wire.

Step 4: Prepare for the swimsuit competition.

Either a one- or two-piece suit is acceptable, but select a suit in a bright solid color or black. Avoid prints or any styles that are too revealing. Four-inch acrylic heels are standard footwear for your walk down the stage.

- Spray Firm Grip to your buttocks before donning your swimsuit to prevent your suit from riding up. (Remove the tacky substance with baby wipes immediately after this portion of the competition; otherwise, you may find yourself stuck to a toilet seat and unable to spring into action.)
- When standing on stage, place one leg in front of the other,

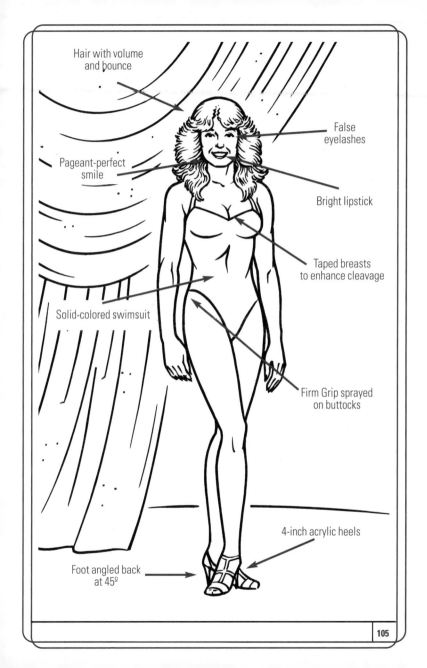

Hair with volume
and bounce

False
eyelashes

Pageant-perfect
smile

Bright lipstick

Taped breasts
to enhance cleavage

Solid-colored swimsuit

Firm Grip sprayed
on buttocks

4-inch acrylic heels

Foot angled back
at 45º

pointing the front foot straight ahead and angling the back foot at 45 degrees to create a flattering, crotch-hiding pose. (With a simple shift of the rear foot to a 90-degree angle, you will be in perfect position to draw your weapon or spin into a roundhouse kick.)

Step 5: Choose an evening gown that flatters your figure but conceals your weapon.

For the evening gown competition, your gown should be form-fitting and loaded with rhinestones or beads. Any color is acceptable. Use duct tape to attach your weapon to your thigh so that it is not visible through your skirt or your skirt's slit.

Step 6: Choose a conservative outfit for the interview portion of the competition.

Don a skirt suit in a solid color with coordinating pumps.

Step 7: Ace the interview.

You should display a general knowledge of current events, voice no controversial opinions, and speak passionately and personally about your platform. Avoid the temptation to display your thorough knowledge of the criminal justice system, Tae Kwon Do, or electronics.

Step 8: Secure your crown, but be ready to bolt.

If you win the pageant and are required to wear a crown, you may need to chase down a suspect in your queenly regalia: remove the crown or tiara to eliminate wind resistance and extra weight, and hike up or rip off your long skirt or train to increase mobility.

When you need to reach an operative who frequents a house of ill repute, you'll have to blend in with the other "working girls."

Step 1: Develop a backstory.

To fit in, develop a false history about yourself and your experience in the industry. For example, if you're young enough to look the part, say you're working your way through college. Be careful about claiming to have worked at other ranches/brothels—the community is fairly tight-knit. Your best bet is to claim that you are just getting started in the business. You may even find a mentor to glom onto.

Step 2: Pack several wardrobe and makeup choices.

Successful "working girls" know that not every client likes the same style of hooker. Options include, but are not limited to: the schoolgirl, the streetwalker, and the upper-class woman. Pack a school uniform, some thigh-high boots, and simulated pearls; you can improvise your wardrobe from there.

Step 3: Establish a sexy one-word name and persona.

Select a name that fits the persona and backstory you have created for yourself—Sunny, Destiny, Star, or Octavia are all viable options.

Step 4: When you arrive at the house, exude a positive attitude.

As the saying goes, "Looks count, but attitude means more." Be friendly and outgoing toward all you come in contact with.

Step 5: Bond with the other employees.

Many of the veteran employees will be watching you initially—

how you work, negotiate with clients, and bond with the other women in the house. Be a good listener, and be open about sharing your (invented) life story.

Step 6: When summoned, line up correctly for a client in the parlor area.
When a client wants to see his choices, you and the other employees should proceed to the parlor. If you want to improve your chances that a client selects you—since he is your undercover target—smile and make constant seductive eye contact.

Step 7: Alternatively, approach a client at the bar.
When a client wants to relax before making a selection, he may choose to sit at the bar. Approach him and speak with him for only 10 minutes. If he does not attempt negotiation, you should clear the way for another employee.

Step 8: Do not accept money from a client unless you are able to follow through on the transaction.
You may negotiate with a client and retire to a room without obligation. If you have not heard the information you are after by now, this is the time to withdraw. Before accepting any money, suggest that there is another employee who may better suit his needs. While you are waiting for the other employee to arrive, suggest he ready himself by removing his pants and freshening up in the bathroom. Examine the contents of his wallet, pants, or briefcase while he is out of the room.

AS A MAN

When deciding upon your disguise, try to emulate what you think looks good on a man. Choose facial features and clothing that you like. You will feel more comfortable and confident.

Step 1: Hide your breasts.

If you are busty, wrap several six-inch-wide Ace bandages around your chest to de-emphasize your breasts. If you have small breasts, forgo the bandages and tape your breasts instead: Using gaffers or athletic tape, start the tape at the nipple and pull each breast to the side. Break off the tape underneath your armpit. Layer your clothing so the bandages and tape are completely hidden. Wear a T-shirt or tank top and then add another shirt over it. Complete the subterfuge with a jacket or blazer.

Step 2: Create a bulge.

While a rolled-up sock can create a bulge, you can also purchase a realistic cyberskin penis (from a sex toys shop or website) that will situate realistically in men's briefs. Your bulge should be set off slightly to the right or left. Avoid anything that will give your new appendage a long, rigid appearance. For underwear, stick to briefs to help hold in your fake bulge. If you are curvy or voluptuous, wear loose or baggy pants over your briefs. If you are narrow-hipped, you can wear more fitted jeans or pants.

Step 3: Alter your features with your mascara wand.

Darken eyebrows and stipple in stubble on your cheeks and chin.

Step 4: Add sideburns, a mustache, goatee, or beard.

Select strips of fake hair that match your skin tone. Hair that contrasts sharply with your skin will draw attention to your disguise. Attach the strips with liquid latex.

Long hair
secured under hat

Realistic
facial hair

Layered clothing
to hide breasts

Realistic
crotch bulge

Assume a manly posture when out in public.

Step 5: Wear a hat.

If you have long hair, secure it in a topknot or high bun, then crush a hat firmly on top of your head. If you have short hair, wear a baseball cap.

Step 6: Modulate your voice and adopt more masculine diction.

Sustaining a lower-pitched voice for an entire evening is nearly impossible, so simply try to tone down your voice and pepper your conversation with common masculine phrases and words, such as "What's up?," "dude," and "man." Listen more than you talk.

Step 7: Walk confidently.

Take up more physical space by swinging your arms and striding. Charge through crowded areas without pausing.

Step 8: When drinking, swig—do not sip—your beverage.

Order beer or something harder than your favorite wine, such as bourbon or a Manhattan. Avoid spritzers.

Step 9: Rehearse.

Practice walking, talking, eating, smoking, and any other behavior you want to add to your disguise. Create a backstory for your character's life to help you stay in character. Tape record your performance or try to trick your friends by leaving them phone messages in your manly persona.

HOW TO MAINTAIN A SECRET IDENTITY

Will Tippen (Bradley Cooper): *Who would live a double life like that?*
Double Agent Sydney Bristow (Jennifer Garner): *There are people....*
    —*Alias*

It is not unusual for an action heroine to be called upon to maintain a secret identity to protect herself and those around her. Courageous women through the ages have donned disguises, spun webs of deception, and led double lives all in the name of justice. Whether you need to be two, three, or many different people—or you want to become another person altogether—you must start with the basics: a birth certificate. Former FBI agent Elvin Keith and security specialist Shawn Engbrecht provide the details.

Step 1: Obtain a false birth certificate.

Comb through a graveyard in a rural area and find a headstone for a female of your ethnicity, born near your actual birth year, who died in infancy. Go to the county clerk (if you have a choice, look for an older female clerk with a trustworthy appearance) and ask for a copy of "your" (i.e., the dead infant's) birth certificate. If the clerk appears suspicious, simply say that your mother had your original certificate but lost it in a move or nasty divorce. If you can create a story that plays on the clerk's sympathy, by all means do so.

Step 2: Gather other forms of identification.

Apply for a driver's license, registration, Social Security number, bank account, and credit cards in your new name, and establish residency at a new apartment. Use cash or money orders to procure your new identification, accounts, apartment, and a car.

Step 3: Create a new background that is close to your real one.

Keep the lie close to the truth, particularly when it involves your background and personal history. If you grew up in a suburb of Dallas, select a different suburb or town close to Dallas as your hometown. If you are a writer, say you worked at a magazine as a copywriter or editor. The more truthful you are, the easier it will be for you to carry out your dual identities. If you create a web of lies, you will have a hard time remembering your cover story. Talk about your background as little as possible.

Step 4: Change your appearance.

A few physical alterations can help you carry out your ruse. Use wigs of different colors and cuts to disguise your real identity. You do not need to make major alterations, but small changes by degrees will help to keep you under everyone's radar.

The more inconspicuous your clothing, the less likely anyone will give you a second look. Think drab. In bright environments, wear pastels and beiges. On dark days or in low-lit interiors, wear darker colors and jeans. With small additions like sunglasses and a hat, you will go unnoticed outdoors.

Step 5: Live and breathe your cover role.

Any slip-up in accent, conversation, appearance, or behavior could spell the end of the action heroine road for you. Patronize different restaurants, bars, and shops than you do in your real life to further avoid detection. Take care not to adopt a new persona and lifestyle that goes against your nature. If you are a homebody and create an identity that includes lots of socializing, it will be difficult to maintain the ruse.

Step 6: If you need to maintain multiple aliases simultaneously, keep your lives as separate as possible.

Take care not to mix up your different personas: Switch your cars at various hotel parking lots. Have two purses stocked for each persona. Keep all your identification in the proper bag and stow the other in the trunk of your second car or another safe spot when not in use. Leave work "at the office" so you will be less likely to carry suspicious paperwork or evidence of your other life. Carry two cell phones and give out your numbers sparingly.

Step 7: Trust no one.

You can maintain dual or multiple identities if you are self-sufficient and without accomplices or confidantes. Do not talk about your real work or identity unless you absolutely know the person can be trusted. You could put others in harm's way if you divulge too much.

If you must correspond with someone covertly, use computers at Internet cafes or photocopy centers and communicate via message boards on predetermined random websites. Establish code names, as well as a code, for relaying information.

John Hammond (Richard Attenborough): *It ought to be me going . . .*
Dr. Ellie Sattler (Laura Dern): *Why?*
John: *Well, I'm a . . . and you're uh, a . . .*
Ellie: *Look, we can discuss sexism in survival situations when I get back.*
    —Jurassic Park

While action heroes may hate asking for directions, heroines are only too happy to ask for assistance. Problem is, in the jungle, there's no one to ask—unless you happen to stumble into a ripped ape-man in a loincloth. You're going to have to hunt, gather, make fire, build a shelter, and seek out water with nothing more than your two hands and steely resolve (and a few trusty items from your handbag). Armed with the following instructions provided by survival expert "Mountain" Mel Deweese, you will find your way out of the wild in no time.

Step 1: Adopt a survival mentality.

Recognize what you are up against and know that you can do whatever it takes to survive. Focus on obtaining fire, shelter, food, water, signals, and first aid. The importance of these six components will rotate constantly, based on your situation, time of day, and geographic location.

Step 2: Light and maintain a fire.

Choose a location that is protected from the elements. Gather twigs, birds' nests, or any small, dry brush to use as tinder. Cotton balls or tissue smeared with petroleum jelly are also excellent fire aids that you can add to the bed of tinder. Concentrate the sunlight onto tinder with the reflective lens of your flashlight. Softly blow onto the sparking fuel until the tinder catches fire. Protect the flame by

CARRY A SURVIVAL KIT

These unassuming action heroine items can save your life.

- **Lip balm and petroleum jelly products for fire aid**

- **Hand sanitizer, cigarettes, and perfume for fire aid**

- **Tissue paper and cotton balls for fire tinder**

- **Matches or cigarette lighter for fire making**

- **String to make fire, use in a trap, or use as fishing line**

- **Safety pins or paper clips to fashion into a fish hook**

- **Scarf or hankie to create a water filter and container**

- **Sponge for collecting water**

- **Mirror for signaling**

- **Condom (when encased in a sock) to serve as a waterproof container for matches or canteen**

A few other essentials probably not tucked away in your handbag:

- **Baggies to collect water and keep matches and clothes dry**

- **Knife**

- **Flashlight**

- **Two lightweight, packable tarps and/or rain ponchos for shelter and collecting water**

nestling small twigs around the tissue. Add small twigs to the fire, then larger twigs, and finally larger pieces of wood. Stoke the fire periodically to maintain it.

Step 3: Seek shelter.

Create your shelter close to your fire-making supplies to conserve as much energy as possible. Shelters should be basic, simple, and quick. Look for natural shelters, such as trees or rocky overhangs. If you have an animal with you, send it into a cave or crevice first to make sure the space is free of wild animals.

If you cannot find a natural shelter, construct a makeshift waist-high bamboo platform to get yourself up off the ground. (In the jungle, rats, pythons, and monitor lizards are just a few of the creatures that come out at night.) Choose dry standing or leaning bamboo, and check that no insects are inside. With a good knife, cut 10 to 20 pieces, each several feet long. Drive 4 stalks into the ground at the 4 corners of a 3- x 6-foot rectangle. Lash the stalks with vines to nearby trees. Lay the remaining poles over the 4 posts to create a table-like platform to lie on, using vines to lash the poles to each other and to surrounding trees as necessary. Stretch a poncho or tarp over the top of the platform to repel rain.

Step 4: Forage and gather food.

Erase any food prejudices you may have.

A few rules:

- Never eat in the same area where you sleep.
- Roast insects to get rid of parasites.
- Avoid any plants with a milky sap.
- Never eat anything with a parsley-like top.
- If it tastes bitter, do not ingest it.
- Blue and black berries are okay for eating.
- Red berries may not be okay; proceed with caution.
- White or green berries should never be eaten.
- Never eat wild mushrooms.

If you are able to trap some game, be sure to kill it before removing it from the trap. Skin the animal. Check the liver for spots to make sure the animal is not diseased before eating. Remove all entrails, cut meat into chunks, skewer the chunks with the end of a stick, and roast thoroughly over a fire.

Step 5: Find and extract water.

Make a high cut into a water vine and then cut it again three feet below the first cut. Water will flow out. Do not touch the vine to your mouth, and beware of any milky or white sap.

Step 6: Learn your surroundings.

Select a sturdy walking stick about 4 or 5 feet in length. Sharpen the end and harden it with fire. Carry your stick to detect snakes or soft ground; it can also double as a spear. Stuff your boots with juniper leaves to repel snakes while walking. Make a bigger and bigger circle each day as you explore your environs, and leave markers so you can keep track of where you've been.

Step 7: Create a signal if you want to be rescued.

Anything that provides a contrast to your natural surroundings can act as a signal. Cut 4- to 5-foot-long poles and peel off the bark to show the pale inner color. Float the poles in a blue lake for contrast.

A mirror is also an effective signal device. Extend your left arm up and look through two fingers. Hold your mirror in your right hand near your cheek. When you see an airplane pass through your fingers, simultaneously aim the mirror so it reflects the sun between your two fingers. You will create a glint that the airplane can see for up to 70 miles.

HOW TO DEAL WITH A GORILLA IN THE MIST

Action heroines might be second only to flight attendants when it comes to racking up travel miles. But rather than dishing out honey-roasted peanuts, an action heroine has to fend off beasts of all kinds in both the urban jungle and the wild kingdom. Whether you're in the jungles of the Congo, your local zoo, or at a trendy new restaurant with a knuckle-dragging date, it is helpful to know the essentials of primate behavior, courtesy of the Philadelphia Zoo's Andy Baker.

Step 1: Identify the species of ape.

When confronted by an ape in the wild, first identify the particular species before attempting to gauge its behavior.

Apes, unlike monkeys, do not have tails. The species are generally divided into "great apes" and "lesser apes."

Among the great apes:
- Gorillas, the biggest of the primates, have black fur and small ears. They can be found in equatorial Africa.
- Orangutans have long, orange fur and are found only on the islands of Sumatra and Borneo.
- Chimpanzees have brownish to black fur and large ears and live in equatorial Africa.

Gibbons are considered the only "lesser apes." They also lack tails but are much smaller than any of the other apes. They can be black, blond, gray, or brown depending on species and gender.

Step 2: Do not approach the ape or make any sudden movements.

Attempt to look small and non-threatening. Crouch, squat, or sit, and do whatever you can to diminish your presence. If you have big hair, hide it under a scarf.

Step 3: Avoid eye contact with the ape.

Apes may regard a stare as a threat. Remove eyeglasses; they amplify the eye area, which you are trying to de-emphasize. Put your head down and take quick glances to keep your eye on it.

Step 4: Do not offer the ape food.

Offering an ape food may only agitate it, as it is confronted with the dilemma of having to approach you—the enemy—to get it.

Step 5: Do not approach a baby gorilla, orangutan, or chimp, no matter how cute it may be.

Apes are most likely to become agitated or aggressive if you come between an adult and its offspring. If you see one ape—small or large—there are probably more nearby. Orangutans are the most solitary of the great apes, so you may run into only one at a time.

If a gorilla or chimp sits down and shoves itself against you, pick through its fur as if you are looking for vermin.

GAUGING APE BEHAVIOR

Observe the ape carefully to determine its mood and intent.

- When upset, gorillas emit a stronger body odor. If one is standing on all fours with stiff arms and legs and clenching its lips tightly together, it may be getting ready to charge. Even if a gorilla charges toward you, however, it will likely veer off before reaching you, so remain calm. Do not move from your current position. Wait until it backs off and you can slowly back away without turning around. When out of the gorilla's view, high-tail it out of the area.

- A droopy lip, in contrast, is a sign of a relaxed gorilla. In this case, you may continue observing the gorilla and slowly move closer.

- If a gorilla beats its chest or bears its teeth, it could be excited, playful, or trying to threaten you. Stay still and wait for additional behavioral cues, or back away from the ape and vacate the area.

- If a chimp or gorilla sits down and shoves itself against you, it may be asking to be groomed. Pick through its fur as if you are looking for vermin. Pick at whatever the ape shoves up against you by separating the fur with one hand and pulling lightly with the other. As long as the ape feels its fur being manipulated, it will be content. Take care not to pull its fur too hard.

- A chimp might puff up its fur, charge around and break things, or hoot and holler if annoyed. Do not move, speak, or attempt to get closer. The chimp will move away when it tires.

- Orangutans are often the hardest of the apes to read. They are usually nondemonstrative. When irritated, they might swing around, puff up their fur, break things, or make a sound called a "kiss squeak." While it will not aim at you when throwing objects, you may want to protect yourself by vacating the area immediately. Back away from the orangutan to quiet it down; the noise it makes may alert others to your presence in the area.

Step 6: Once you have completed your observations, vacate the area.

Slowly stand up, but remain slightly hunched over to stay small. Keep your head down and take only quick glances at the ape as you slowly back away until you are out of sight. Once the coast is clear, hasten your exit and get on with your work.

CHAPTER 4
Brawn Skills

ACTION HEROINES MAY not have the same muscle mass as their male counterparts, but they sure as heck make up for it in fitness, efficient fat-burning, and sheer will. Taking a cue from Sarah Connor, the savvy heroine knows the benefits of bulking up. Besides, the visual benefit of looking great in tank tops, cut arms, a six-pack, and muscular legs are serious tools in the action heroine's bag of tricks. (And working out is a productive way to while away the time if you have been wrongly institutionalized.)

But it's not just about bulging biceps. You can use every part of your buff body to bring down villains. You can choke a bounty hunter with your thighs of steel. You can take down a villainess with a few boxing basics and a whole lot of creative accessorizing. If lost in the matrix or backed into a corner, you can run up the wall and fell the enemy with a well-placed kick. With a flick of your strong yet supple wrist, you can whip their hides. If you are feeling generous, you can offer your opponent a handicap by cuffing your hands behind your back before you flatten him.

If all else fails and you happen to be a traditionalist, just go for the classic knee to the groin. He'll be begging you for mercy in no time.

HOW TO WIN A CATFIGHT

Amanda Woodward (Heather Locklear): *If I have to watch Alison strut her traitorous butt across the courtyard, I'm gonna kill one of us.*
   —*Melrose Place*

Whether you are taking someone down for stealing your man or scratching out a coworker's eyes for stealing your idea, it is handy to know how to master the catfight. Sharpening your jungle-red talons is only a small part of good catfight technique; according to stuntwoman Danielle Burgio, you also have to be prepared to protect vulnerable areas on your body. The most important thing to bring to the brawl, however, is the will to win. Victory (and maybe even the hunky man across the courtyard) will be indisputably yours.

Step 1: Prepare to use anything and everything on your person as a weapon.

The more tricked out you are, the better, so remember to accessorize.

- Heels, jewelry, rings, and long fingernails can all be used to cut, scratch, and bruise your opponent's face.
- A belt can be used as a whip.
- The bow of your sunglasses or your spiky heels can be used to jab.

Step 2: Take steps to protect yourself.

Put your hair up and out of the way to avoid a vicious hair-pulling. Be prepared to assume the proper fighting stance to defend your face and chest (see "How to Take a Hit in the Boobs," opposite).

Step 3: Plan your offensive punches.

If you are shorter than the enemy, body punches are the way to go. If you tower over your opponent, use an uppercut to the chin.

Step 4: Take your enemy off guard.

Offer to resolve the dispute peacefully through conversation. When she begins to calm down and listen to reason, proceed to deliver a sucker punch to the chin or abdomen.

Step 5: Deliver the punch.

Keep your body tight and step into your punches if you can, while slightly torquing or twisting your hips.

To deliver an uppercut, make a fist with your thumb on the outside. Draw your arm back slightly, then bring your fist up and squarely make contact underneath your opponent's chin.

HOW TO TAKE A HIT IN THE BOOBS AND OTHER DEFENSES

Even the most seasoned action heroines get knocked around from time to time. Perhaps the most painful blow to take, however, is having your breasts hit or mashed unexpectedly. If your breasts have been enhanced or are otherwise tender, take extra care when fighting. Former world champion boxer Jill Matthews advises wearing a supportive sports bra (avoid underwires that could puncture the skin) and keeping your arms in a boxer's stance throughout the brawl.

Step 1: Keep your opponent at arm's length at all times.
The closer your opponent gets, the more force she can apply to a boob blow.

Step 2: Assume the proper boxer's stance.
With your elbows bent and in front of your chest, hold your fists in front of your face at about eyebrow level. This will help protect your torso, specifically your boobs. Look through your hands at your opponent to maintain visual contact.

Step 3: Dodge or step away from the blow.
A glancing blow is better than full contact. If you are about to be hit in the right breast, for example, take one step back with your right foot and move with the momentum of the punch. Do not stand still and brace yourself against the blow.

Step 4: Take steps to reduce your discomfort when the fight is over.
To reduce swelling and pain, remove your bra and apply a cold pack to the injured area. Take ibuprofin to alleviate any pain.

To punch her in the abdomen, begin with your elbows in and close to your body. Stepping into the punch, quickly jab your dominant fist either straight out or angled slightly down (depending on your opponent's height) until you make solid contact with her body.

Step 6: Continue to deliver body blows.

Aim for any area around the waist, such as the kidneys, which are located on the back of the body a few inches above each hip. A good punch to the boobs will hurt her as well. If her hair is long, pull it . . . hard. Use your fingernails or rings to claw her face. Pull off a shoe and jab her in the arm. Whip her with your belt.

Step 7: Avoid inflicting injuries that might bring legal action.

Hair-pulling, body blows, and light scratching will most likely not get you community service or jail time; breaking someone's nose will (unless it's in self-defense).

Step 8: Stay on the offensive.

If you can, wrestle your opponent to the ground or back her into a corner by continuing to move forward. She will be off balance and forced to back up until she's literally up against the wall.

Step 9: Once your opponent is sufficiently incapacitated or has run away, get to safety.

HOW TO CHOKE A MAN WITH YOUR BARE THIGHS

Xenia Onatopp (Famke Janssen): *You don't need the gun.*
James Bond (Pierce Brosnan): *Well, that depends on your definition of safe sex.*
   —Goldeneye

Every action heroine worth her salt knows how to use every part of her body to fend off a foe. When wrapped around a man's neck or abdomen, a pair of killer thighs can be as effective as any weapon in capturing a man's attention. This maneuver can be performed almost anywhere and in virtually any ensemble—though short skirts or stretchy leggings are preferable. Whether you have the strength of a replicant with thighs of steel or you are working overtime in a steam room as a sultry Russian agent, it pays to know how to take a man's breath away . . . literally. Here's how, according to jujitsu expert Robert Hodgkin.

FROM A STANDING POSITION

Step 1: Knock your opponent to his knees.

Your opponent should be on all fours, in what is commonly known as "doggie style." To bring your opponent to the floor, use either of the following techniques:

- Kick your opponent in the back, between the shoulder blades, so that he falls to the floor.
- Stand behind your opponent. Place one foot in front of his feet and push him forward, essentially tripping him over your foot and to the ground.

Of course, you can also suggest sexual relations with your opponent and ask him to assume the position voluntarily.

Step 2: Straddle your opponent's neck between your thighs.

Step or jump over your opponent's shoulders so that his head is between your thighs. As you land over your opponent's head and neck, run your fingers through his hair, grab a clump, and pull his head firmly back to expose his neck. Close your legs around his neck by pressing them together at the knees. The initial jolt of your landing will help you secure his neck. Do not sit on your opponent's back. Remain standing as you proceed to step 3.

Step 3: Quickly release pressure for an instant to assume a position with more solid footing.

As you release, lower yourself so that your opponent's neck is fitted securely under your pelvis. Bend slightly at the knees, flatten your feet for solid footing, and bring your feet closer together.

Step 4: Reapply pressure by squeezing at the knees.

With a swift motion, press your thighs tightly together. Extend your arms as needed for balance.

Step 5: Straighten your knees to take your opponent off balance.

Continue to deliver pressure inward and stand up. This will raise your opponent slightly from the floor and take away any leverage he might have.

Step 6: Box your opponent's ears to keep him subdued.

Extend your arms slightly in front of your body into a "T" formation, with your palms open and facing the floor. Bring your hands down and together onto your opponent's ears—as if you were clapping and your opponent's head just happened to be in the way.

Step 7: Pull his chin toward your head.

Wrap both of your hands under his chin and pull firmly upward. This will keep your opponent locked firmly in place between your thighs.

Step 8: Hold this position until your opponent falls unconscious or is stunned enough for you to escape.

FROM A PRONE POSITION

To choke a man with your bare thighs from a prone position, your opponent should be standing over you. Lie on your back with your legs bent at the knees and your feet flat on the floor.

Step 1: Use both hands to grab your opponent at the bicep and chest.

Grab either loose clothing (shirt or jacket) or actual muscle (if your opponent is in a tight shirt or stripped down). With your left hand, grab onto the outside of your opponent's right arm, between the shoulder and the elbow. With your right hand, grab your opponent at the chest—about the second button down from the neck.

Step 2: With your left foot, lock your opponent at the hip.

Insert your left foot into your opponent's right hip. It should fit snugly as your opponent stands bent forward. Keep your foot firmly pressed against the hip to secure your opponent in place.

Step 3: With your right foot, deliver three swift kicks to your opponent's groin.

This should further disable your opponent—unless he is wearing a protective cup or is lacking certain "equipment."

Step 4: Raise your right leg straight up between your opponent's head and your right arm.

To choke a man from a prone position:

1. Grab opponent at the bicep and chest.

2. Kick him in the groin.

3. Bring your right leg between his head and your right arm.

4. Bring his right torso to your left thigh.

5. Lock your legs around his neck.

Step 5: Bring your opponent's neck down to your right thigh.

Kick your opponent's hip out with your left foot (already in position) while simultaneously pulling your opponent into place with your arms. The left side of his neck should be on the inside of your right thigh, and his left shoulder should be immobilized.

Step 6: Bring your opponent's right torso to your left thigh.

Be sure to clear your left leg so that it is outside of—and not underneath—your opponent. Pull his right arm down to your chest. His right armpit should be pinned on the inside of your left thigh.

Step 7: Lock your legs around your opponent's neck and arm.

Bend your right leg at the knee across the top of his shoulders and the back of his neck. Raise your left leg and bend it over your right ankle so that your knee locks your legs together.

Step 8: Secure your opponent's right arm.

Wrap your left arm over your opponent's right arm and secure it under your armpit. This will prevent him from being able to gouge, scratch, or fight back.

Step 9: Squeeze your hips and thighs together to render your opponent unconscious.

HOW TO SUBDUE YOUR OPPONENT WITH A WHIP

Catwoman (Michelle Pfeiffer): *I am Catwoman. Hear me roar.*
—*Batman Returns*

At first blush, it may seem like overkill. How often, after all, do you read about a purse snatcher being caught by a babe with a bullwhip or a wild beast being stopped in its tracks by the sting of a 12-footer? But as the seasoned action heroine knows, the whip isn't just a fancy weapon. It's as sexy (especially when you're wearing a lycra cat-suit) as it is versatile. In a pinch it can be used as a rope to hang from or climb up; as a tourniquet; or even as a cord for tying up the bad guy. Here's how to crack that whip, according to stuntwoman Danielle Burgio.

Step 1: Wait for your opponent to enter your fighting range.
Once he is within 10 feet of you, ready your whip.

CHOOSING A WHIP

Whips come in different lengths, but a 12-foot whip is the best choice for cracking and wrapping. Shorter whips, like riding crops, can be used to inflict pain or control a subject at a closer distance. If you can, purchase an Australian Kangaroo whip, which cracks loudly and is extremely accurate, due to its many plaits. With a 12-foot whip, you will need 8 to 10 feet of distance between yourself and your target. Work on developing an eye for judging distance; it will be extremely important for fighting effectively.

Step 2: Keep your opponent at bay by cracking the lash in front of his body.

The number one rule when cracking a whip is to make sure that the palm holding the whip is always facing away from your body.

- Circle the whip over your head. Keep the whip as far above your head as you can, while still allowing for smooth whip movement. If the whip is in your right hand, swing it counterclockwise. If it's in your left, swing it clockwise. Keep your back straight and your elbow slightly bent to ensure a smooth motion. Keep your opposite arm out to give you balance and style.
- Make one large circle overhead, and then a quick upright S approximately two feet in front of you, keeping your wrist loose and your palm away from you. The S should start facing upward, as if you're writing on the ceiling. Position your wrist at a 45-degree angle to your body as you bring the whip down and complete the S motion. Wherever you follow through with your wrist is where the tip—the most dangerous part of the whip—will go.

Step 3: Lash the whip around your opponent's chest and arms.

Circle your whip overhead to gain momentum, then throw it out to the side with your arm extending and your wrist facing away from you. Use your other arm to maintain your balance. Hit your opponent on his side with the middle of the whip's lash. The rest of the whip will circle around him and secure his arms and torso.

Step 4: With the whip taut, take your opponent to the ground.

With a firm grip on the whip, place one of your feet behind your opponent's heel, then trip him back over your leg by pushing him from the chest. Keep him on his back to restrict his leg movement.

Step 5: Immobilize your opponent by tying him up with rope.

To subdue your opponent with a whip:

1. Circle the whip over your head in a counterclockwise direction.

2. Make a swift S-shape with your wrist as you crack the whip.

3. Hit your foe on his side with the middle of the whip.

4. Hold the whip taut as it circles around his torso.

HOW TO FIGHT WITH YOUR HANDS CUFFED

Dylan (Drew Barrymore): *By the time this is over, every one of you is gonna be face down on the floor. And since my trusty lighter isn't working, I'm gonna do all of this with my hands tied behind my back.*
    —Charlie's Angels

While there might be a couple of situations where being handcuffed could be considered a good thing, you usually want your hands free to hunt, gather, and generally whoop ass. But if you do find yourself facing the bad guy with your wrists manacled, don't worry: You can still manage to inflict some pain on one, two, or a passel of thugs. Come to think of it your body is such a powerful instrument that it's only polite to give the underdogs a small handicap every now and again. Here's how, according to security expert Shawn Engbrecht.

To increase your effectiveness before fighting with your hands cuffed:
- Pull your shirt or coat sleeves down before you are cuffed. The handcuffs will be looser when you pull up the sleeves.
- Draw your hand toward the cuff as it is being closed. This will cause the cuff to close over the meaty portion of your hand (above where the wrist meets the hand). Slip the cuffs back down toward your wrist once they are closed and they should be looser.

WITH YOUR HANDS BEHIND YOU

With your hands cuffed behind you, your arms are unavailable for fighting. You must use the tools you have available—head, teeth, knees, legs, and feet—as weapons instead.

Step 1: Kick your opponent in the throat.

While facing your opponent, deliver a vertical kick to his throat. Point your toe so that it lands on your opponent's esophagus. Secure your weight on your back foot as you kick.

Alternatively, brace the foot that is furthest from your opponent flat on the ground. Deliver a sideways but vertical kick to your opponent's throat. Flatten your foot so that your heel lands on your opponent's esophagus.

Step 2: Knee your opponent in the groin.

As your opponent recovers from the blow, deliver a full-force, upward-moving knee to your opponent's groin. This is an effective move for an opponent of either sex, although the effects are usually longer lasting on male opponents.

Step 3: Head butt your opponent over the bridge of his nose.

As your opponent rises from his doubled-over position, tighten and straighten your back, neck, and head—as if your spine were a solid, flat board. Step toward your opponent and bend forward at the waist. Use the high section of your forehead to deliver the head butt onto the bridge of your opponent's nose. This may render him unconscious or at least thoroughly bloodied.

Step 4: Bite your opponent's nose or ear.

Your front teeth are sharper and will break skin more quickly.

Step 5: Bring your hands in front of you to "slip" the cuffs.

Lie flat on your back. Bring your hands down past your buttocks, slipping them one at a time past your hips. Bring your legs, one at a time, through your arms so that they are in front of you.

To fight with your hands cuffed:

1. Kick your opponent in the throat.

2. Knee him in the groin.

3. Head butt him over the bridge of his nose.

4. Bring your hands in front of you to slip the cuffs.

WITH YOUR HANDS IN FRONT OF YOU

If your opponent has not been rendered unconscious, or your hands are bound in front of you at the outset, use the following techniques.

Step 1: Step behind your opponent so that you are facing his back.

Step 2: Bring your hands over his head and use your cuffs as a garrote.
Cut off your opponent's airway by pulling your cuffed hands toward your body. Continue with steps 3 to 5 in rapid succession.

Step 3: Wedge one knee into your opponent's spine.
With your hands around his neck, pull your arms toward your body while simultaneously pushing the knee of your non-dominant leg into the small of your opponent's lower back. This will take away his leverage.

Step 4: Place your forehead against the back of your opponent's head just above the nape of his neck.
Press your head forward and continue to pull your hands toward you. Your opponent may be flailing his arms furiously, but he will not be able to reach you effectively.

Step 5: Step back and drop to your knees.
With your arms and head still in position, remove your knee from his back and use that leg to take one step back. Drop to your other knee and force your opponent straight to the floor. Hold your arms and head in position until your opponent is rendered unconscious. (This typically takes one to two minutes.)

Step 6: Remove your handcuffs from around your opponent's neck and get to safety.

HOW TO KNOCK OUT A MAN WITH A RUNNING WALL KICK

Lieutenant (Bill Young): *I think we can handle one little girl. I sent two units—they're bringing her down now.*
Agent Smith (Hugo Weaving): *No, Lieutenant, your men are dead.*
　　　　　—The Matrix

While it's nice to be a knockout, it's more important to know how to deliver a knockout kick. Next time you find yourself backed into a corner by zombie dogs or a computer-generated SWAT team, don't just rely on your good looks to get you out of the situation. White Lotus Kung Fu instructor Carrie Wong recommends drawing your adversary into a corner and using the wall to deliver the boot and cold-cock your enemy.

When you're about to be trapped in a corner with no way out, the running wall kick will take your opponent by surprise and put you in prime position for knocking him out with a blow to the neck.

Step 1: Sprint full force toward the corner formed by two walls.
You should have at least 15 to 25 feet between you and the walls so that you can gain enough momentum. Do not get too far ahead of your opponent—if he is more than two steps behind you, slow down slightly. If he is less than two steps behind you, speed up.

Step 2: When you reach the wall, run one step up with your dominant foot.
Plant your foot firmly on the wall at about waist height. If you're right-foot dominant, plant your right foot on the right wall, vis-à-vis the corner; if you're left-foot dominant, plant your left foot on

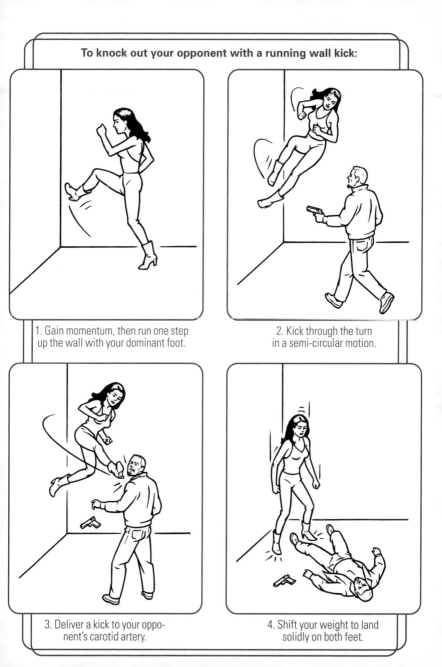

To knock out your opponent with a running wall kick:

1. Gain momentum, then run one step up the wall with your dominant foot.

2. Kick through the turn in a semi-circular motion.

3. Deliver a kick to your opponent's carotid artery.

4. Shift your weight to land solidly on both feet.

the left-hand wall. Lean your weight forward to compensate for your vertical climb. Keep your knee slightly bent.

Step 3: Step up with your non-dominant foot onto the opposite wall.
Plant your second foot on the wall about waist high, but slightly below and diagonal to your dominant foot. Shift your weight naturally as you run up the wall and "around" the corner. Keep your momentum moving forward, leaning your torso toward the ceiling. Keep your knee slightly bent.

Step 4: Turn so that your "open" side spins toward your opponent.
Your open side is on the same side as your non-dominant foot. Your dominant leg should follow your turn and will begin to pull off the wall. Keep your knee bent and your foot flexed.

Step 5: Continue your turn and extend your dominant leg in a circular motion.
Swing your leg through the turn with your leg extended but slightly bent at the knee. Your kick should travel in a semi-circular motion—like a crescent moon.

Step 6: Use your dominant foot to connect with your opponent's throat.
With your foot flexed, deliver a kick such that the flat of your foot connects with your opponent's carotid artery. The carotid arteries run up either side of your opponent's throat. The most vulnerable point is a few inches above the clavicle, about midway up the neck. A solid kick to this area will disrupt your opponent's blood flow and cause him to fall to the floor and/or black out.

Step 7: Shift your weight to land solidly on both feet.
Land with your non-dominant foot first. Bring your dominant foot down in front of your body in a staggered stance.

HOW TO DISARM A KNIFE-WIELDING KILLER

Randy Meeks (Jamie Kennedy): *Careful, this is the moment when the supposedly dead killer comes back for one last scare.*
Sidney Prescott (Neve Campbell): *Not in my movie.*
    —Scream

Knives don't slash heroines. Psycho killers in Halloween and hockey masks slash heroines. Whether the masked assassin comes to the door or calls first, a few well-placed jabs or slashes can spell the end of the road for any heroine, so if at all possible, lock the doors, don't answer the phone, protect your vital areas—and scream whenever you feel the need. According to Sensei Debbie Hamilton, chances are high that you *will* be cut during a knife fight, so if you can't evade your attacker, you must attack and disarm him.

Step 1: Step into the attacker in defensive posture.

Raise your forearms in front of your body so that they protect your stomach, heart, and chest. Watch the blade's trajectory: Before the blade comes across or down, take one step into your attacker so that you are inside the path of the knife.

Step 2: Simultaneously, deliver a brachial stun to your opponent's neck.

Raise the arm that is farthest away from your opponent's knife arm. If the attacker is slashing from left to right, use your left arm, and vice versa. Deliver a blow to the side of your opponent's neck, at the base just above the clavicle. Use a fist with your middle knuckle protruding above the rest, or the meat of your open hand (pinky side) where the hand and wrist attach.

EVERYDAY KNIFE DEFENSES

- Keep a chair in front of your body, leg side toward your attacker, to defend against the knife's blade.

- Throw a bed sheet over your opponent to temporarily blind or confuse him, and make your escape.

- Throw heavy garbage cans at your attacker's feet to keep him at bay and off balance.

Step 3: Control your attacker by grabbing his neck and the wrist of the knife hand.
Slide the hand that delivered the brachial stun around the back of your opponent's neck. Grasp his neck firmly in your palm. Simultaneously, slide your opposite hand down to the wrist of your attacker's knife hand. Grasp firmly, with your palm facing away from you, to keep the blade away from your body.

Step 4: Quickly move several steps backward and take your attacker to the floor.
As you step backward, keep a firm, downward pressure on both the opponent's neck and knife hand. Force him face-first to the ground.

Step 5: Pin your attacker's arms with your knees.
Drop your knees onto his biceps while continuing to hold his knife hand. You will be straddling your attacker's back. Press both of your knees into his biceps to immobilize them.

Step 6: Disarm your attacker.
Use one or both of your hands to grab the knife from the butt side and pry it out toward the tips of his thumb and forefinger.

Step 7: Run to safety.
Be sure to secure the knife by holding it in your hand at a 90-degree angle, pointing away from your body.

CHAPTER 5
Escape Skills

NO MATTER HOW tired you may be from all your crime fighting, the credits can't roll until you've successfully evaded all dangers—natural as well as manmade. Before you can officially become a franchise and have your own action figure, you're going to have to bust a move to bust out of your tight spot.

Along the way, don't be surprised if you have to climb into a pickup truck with an ex-husband you still secretly love to outdistance a tornado, or perhaps fake a drowning to dupe your psycho husband. And all too many heroines have had to deal with an overly attentive trucker while roadtripping with a girlfriend.

Then there are the less conventional predicaments that require a clean getaway. You may need to elude a Casanova kidnapper or a bazooka-toting baddie. You might have to pilot a helicopter without the aid of Keanu Reeves. You might even be called upon to mount a horse and courier a hobbit to safety.

A true action heroine never can be too prepared to evade danger. So read on and learn how to make a graceful—or at least speedy—exit on foot, by car, by raft, on horseback, and even in a helicopter.

Laura Burney (Julia Roberts): *That was the night that I died, and someone else was saved. Someone who was afraid of water, but learned to swim. Someone who knew there'd be one moment when he wouldn't be watching.*
    —*Sleeping with the Enemy*

No one said being an action heroine would be easy, but when it comes time to elude the bad guys by staging your own death, you'll be facing a near-impossible task. To successfully fake your death, your body must be presumed lost at sea. Dredging a large area of water is a difficult and time-consuming task; when your remains are not found within a few days of your disappearance, chances are the authorities will be forced to give up the search. Former FBI agent Elvin Keith and security specialist Shawn Engbrecht provide these helpful instructions.

Step 1: Purchase a boat and familiarize yourself with its operation.
A year in advance of your planned disappearance, purchase a small motor boat (a 10- to 12-footer) and make a big show of taking navigation and boating lessons.

Step 2: Become a capable boater.
Periodically take friends and family out on your watercraft to display your prowess at the helm. Insist that everyone on the boat wear life preservers at all times. Casually tell all on-board that you cannot swim or are not a strong swimmer.

Step 3: Learn how to swim.
Take lessons in a town where you will not be recognized.

Step 4: Create a new identity.

At least six months before you are ready to "die," obtain a fake birth certificate and set up new credit cards and a bank account under your new name (see "How to Maintain a Secret Identity," p. 112) in a town as far away from your current home as possible. Gradually stash $5,000 to $10,000 in your new account. Be prepared to leave behind funds and investments to avoid suspicion.

Step 5: Cover yourself.

Take care not to raise any suspicions. Your financial records, phone logs, and computer activity will be thoroughly examined after your "death."

- As you build funds in your new account, carefully siphon off funds from your original account. Make regular cash withdrawals from ATMs rather than using checks or a debit card.
- Buy a "new" used car with cash.
- Distance yourself from friends and family so that you are not in daily or weekly contact with them.
- If you must make emergency calls, purchase a phone card at a convenience store and use it on pay phones only. Destroy the card when the time has been used up.

Step 6: Keep your "new" car at an inconspicuous location near where your boat is docked.

Fill up the gas tank and store a change of drab-colored clothing in the trunk.

Step 7: Go boating alone on the night of your "death."

When the water is rather rough, plan on taking your boat out several miles from shore. Stow an inflatable kayak, air pump, and paddle on board. Carry supplies with you in a waterproof container, including your new birth certificate and identification, cash, new credit cards, and keys to your new home and car.

Step 8: **Once you are a safe distance from shore, abandon the boat.**
Turn off the engine. Do not drop anchor. Inflate your kayak and place aboard all incriminating evidence as well as your water-proof container of supplies. Board the kayak and quickly paddle away from the boat. The authorities will assume you fell over-board in the choppy water.

Step 9: **Paddle to shore near your new car and deflate your raft.**
Brush away your footprints as you walk backward to your vehicle with your belongings. Change into dry clothing and store every-thing in the trunk of your car.

Step 10: **Assume your new identity immediately.**
Quickly drive to your new hometown and assume your new life.

Step 11: **Lay low.**
If you are used to expensive restaurants and hot dance clubs, adopt a more sedate lifestyle of potlucks and book clubs. You are less likely to be fingered by former acquaintances if you do not patronize busy bars or public spaces. Do not attend parades or public events that are videotaped or televised. Do not root for your former hometown's sports teams. Resist the temptation to look up news of your family and town on the Internet. Instead, immerse yourself in the culture of your new town. Do not contact any friends or family members, and do not return to any places you formerly frequented, no matter how tempted you may be.

HOW TO ESCAPE WHEN KIDNAPPED

Casanova (Cary Elwes): *Don't try to escape. Don't cry out for help. And DO NOT try your kickboxing tricks.*
     —Kiss the Girls

No heroine likes to be trapped, whether she's on a remote island or in the forests of North Carolina. Hostage negotiator Larry Chavez recommends that if you can't wait it out, *get out*. By any means necessary. Once you're free, run hard and don't look back. Your chance will come soon enough to turn the tables and see your captor climbing the walls in a small, windowless room for, say, 10 to 15 years.

Once you are at your captor's chosen location, look for clues to determine whether it's better to risk an escape than to wait for a negotiated resolution to your kidnapper's demands. Key indications that escape is the best option include the following:

- Your captor will not talk to you or call you by name.
- Your captor moves you to a solitary location where he will not have to see or deal with you.
- Your captor shows inappropriate affect or irrational emotion (e.g., he laughs when it would be more appropriate to cry).
- Your captor discusses his own potential suicide.
- Your captor's actions are not consistent (e.g., he will not let you move from room to room after he says you may).

Step 1: Note the room's points of exit and entry.

Examine the immediate area for windows, doors, or ventilation access. If the room has a window, determine if you are above ground level. If the room has a door, note how many locks and on which side the hinges are installed.

Step 2: Observe your surroundings.

Look for telltale clues to your whereabouts. Examine the name and address on a magazine or utility bill to determine where you are. Listen for traffic, trains, foghorns, or airplanes taking off or landing to determine if you are in an urban or rural area. Listen for babies crying or dogs barking to determine what sounds might be activated by your escape attempt.

Step 3: Note your captor's routine and sleeping habits.

Make mental notes of how frequently and consistently your captor enters and leaves the area (or at least the room you are in). If you do not have access to a watch, and if the room has a window, note the relative position of the sun in relation to the environment outside. Observing the degree of shadow or glare on a window or a strip of sunlight as it moves across the floor will help you estimate the time of day.

Step 4: Formulate a plan based on your observations.

Plan to escape when you know your captor will be away or otherwise occupied for a long stretch of time. Choose to exit through the window or door that is most easily accessed. Visualize your surroundings and plot a course for your escape.

Step 5: Break out of the most accessible exit.

- If you are breaking out a window, thrust your foot or a small, heavy object, such as a paperweight or a bookend, directly at the center of the glass. Wrap your elbow or hand in a jacket or shirt and clear the remaining shards from the frame.

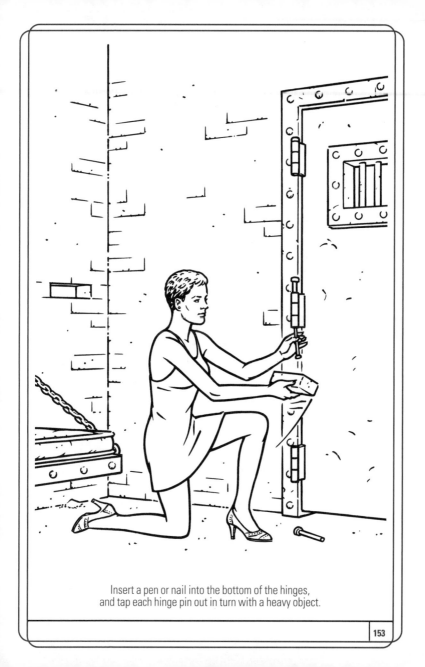

Insert a pen or nail into the bottom of the hinges,
and tap each hinge pin out in turn with a heavy object.

- If breaking out a door, punch through a door panel or remove the hinge pins. If the door has several panels, flatten your foot and deliver a firm kick to the panel nearest the lock and knob. Reach through and unlock and open the door. If the door is solid and the hinges are on your side, insert a stiff pen or nail into the bottom of the top hinge. Kick or tap the hinge pin up and out with your shoe or other firm object. Repeat for each of the remaining hinge pins, then pry the door open.

Step 6: Get outside as quickly as possible.

If you are going out a door, run straight toward an exit sign or the most likely exit to the outdoors. If you are going out a window above ground with no fire escape available, you may need to jump. Aim for a tree, bush, or similar object that may break your fall (see "How to Win a Chase Across Rooftops," p. 173).

Step 7: Get as much distance between you and your captor as possible.

Run to a populated area. If you are in a rural location, get at least two miles away, climb to an elevated position (in a tree or on a hilltop), and look for roads or power lines to lead you toward civilization. Travel parallel to roads, not on them, in case your captor goes looking for you.

Step 8: Use the nearest phone to dial for help.

Alert the authorities to your whereabouts. Use your observations of the area to give them as much information as possible.

HOW TO FEND OFF A SEXUALLY HARASSING TRUCKER

Louise Sawyer (Susan Sarandon): *Where do you get off behaving that way with women you don't even know, huh? How'd you feel if someone did that to your mother or your sister or your wife?*
—Thelma and Louise

You may be used to dealing with admirers, but when they cross that fine line between fan and fanatic, you need to be prepared to haul ass. If you are harassed by a trucker while filling your tank or your tummy at a truck stop, gas station, or rest area, remain calm and in control. He may have a big rig, but that's probably the only sizeable equipment he's packing, so don't let him rile you. Confrontation expert Andrew Netschay and over-the-road trucker Dawn Rodriguez recommend removing yourself from the situation, driving defensively, and making sure you stay on a well-traveled road. In other words, keep on truckin'.

When faced with a sexually harassing trucker, you must use a combination of anti-harassment techniques and defensive driving. One of your greatest advantages is your perceived vulnerability; the harasser does not expect to endure any physical pain as a consequence of attacking you. Your most powerful weapon is your brain and your mouth.

AT A TRUCK STOP

Step 1: Make brief eye contact with as many people as you can when entering the stop.

Many harassers find eye contact intimidating. Minimize your

chances of being harassed by looking in the eyes of as many people as you can. Do not stare anyone down. Instead, briefly scan your surroundings and everyone in that space to arm yourself with valuable tactical information.

Step 2: When harassed, take care of your business quickly and remove yourself from the situation.

Before you exit, look the harasser directly in the eye and tell him to "back off." Alternatively, speak to the attendant and ask him to detain the harasser for 5 minutes.

Step 3: Get in your car and secure it.

Scan the car's interior to ensure that no one is lying in wait in the back seat. Get in the car, roll up the windows, close the sunroof, and lock the doors.

Step 4: Drive away.

If the trucker attempts to stop you from leaving, use a cell phone to dial the authorities. If no cell phone is available, press and hold your horn to draw attention to your situation. If you believe your safety (and/or life) is in danger, start driving, even if it means hitting the harasser.

ON THE ROAD

If the harassment continues onto the road, use the following techniques to fend off the trucker.

Step 1: Stay calm and avoid making eye contact with the trucker.

Ignoring the trucker may end the situation immediately. Your trucker has the upper hand on the road—an eighteen-wheeler—

and confrontation should be avoided at all costs. Make note of the trucker's company and license plate.

Step 2: Slow your vehicle and change lanes.

If you are on the highway, stay at a safe speed (above 55 mph), but slow your vehicle so that the trucker passes you. Change into the slowest outside lane.

Step 3: If the trucker follows your lead, stay in front of his truck.

Speed up as necessary to stay out of the truck's range. You do not want to be in a position where he can push you off the road—with you to the outside lane and the truck next to you.

Step 4: Take evasive action.

Keep yourself at a safe speed in the outside lane. Watch your side mirror for oncoming traffic. Change into the middle lane, and place more vehicles between you and the harassing trucker. Eighteen-wheelers require more time and distance to change lanes, so you should be able to get a sizeable lead.

Step 5: Exit the highway or turn off of the road.

After you exit, wait a few moments for the trucker to get ahead of you and then get back on. If exiting from a standard roadway, be sure not to drive into a blind alley.

Step 6: Drive to a police station or other crowded area.

If you are in unfamiliar territory, drive toward the brightest lights or most heavily trafficked areas. Look for road signs indicating highway patrol, police, or hospital.

Gail (Meryl Streep): *You guys are going to have to throw your weight and high-side it if we wrap around one of these rocks. You're going to have to paddle hard when I tell you. And you're going to have to DO what I say when I say it. Otherwise we got no chance in hell of making it through!*
—*River Wild*

All too often action heroines find themselves confronted with the perilous combination of white water and rednecks. As dangerous a cocktail as they may be, you someday may be forced to guide a crew downriver or paddle solo to outsmart and outmuscle a creepy criminal. It is possible to survive the Gauntlet or navigate Class V+ rapids (the roughest, most technical water to navigate, with severe consequences if you make a mistake). White water veteran Heather Ewing says a well-equipped raft and some advance scouting are absolutely essential if you want to live through the hydraulics, rocks, and drop-offs. Sadly, no amount of planning can predict the actions of a wily redneck. (Cue banjo.)

ENTERING THE WATER

Step 1: Check the air levels of your raft.

Unload your raft to the shore or riverbank. Make sure you have enough air in the raft's chambers. Cold water will contract the air and make your boat softer. The air should be at 3 psi/chamber. If the weather and the water is hot, air will expand, so "bleed" some air (2.5 to 3 psi max). If your raft is overinflated, you risk popping an air chamber.

Step 2: Load your boat.

Pair off people who are the same approximate size. Position two strong paddlers in back and two in front. As the guide, you should climb into the back of the boat if you are in a paddle raft. Climb into the center of the boat and use both oars if you are in an oar raft.

Step 3: Put in your raft in calm water and review crew commands.

Go over paddle commands with your crew: "all forward" (everyone paddling forward), "all back" (everyone paddling backward), "left turn" (passengers on the right should paddle forward, passengers on the left should paddle backward), and "right turn" (passengers on the left should paddle forward, passengers on the right should paddle backward).

MANEUVERING THE RAPIDS

Step 1: Position your raft as it enters the white water.

To avoid flipping, it is important to position your raft perpendicular to large waves or rapids. Attack the water head on by paddling aggressively to increase momentum to shoot you through the rapids quickly and get to the other side. If you cannot line up your raft properly, it is better to enter a rapid backward rather than broadside. Always try to "T" up to a wave. It's nice to see where you are going, but if a wave spins you and suddenly it is easier to square up the back end of your raft instead of spinning around your front, go with the flow. Do not try and fight the river if you get spun. Run with it and make the necessary adjustments.

Step 2: Brace for impact with obstacles.

If you are going to hit a massive rock, aim the nose of your raft right

Position your raft perpendicular to the large waves or rapids.

at it. Brace for impact and instruct your crew to do the same. Hold your paddles firmly and get down into the bottom of the raft. You should pinball off the rock. (See "Capsizing and Rescue Tips," opposite.)

Step 3: Brace for severe drops.

If you are forced to raft down an abrupt drop of more than a few feet, paddle aggressively. As you hit the drop, move to the bottom of the boat and hold on. Optimally, the rapid will spit you out at the bottom. Be aware that head or spinal injuries could result from such a drop, or that you or your raft could be pinned at the base of the waterfall or rapid by the weight of the rushing water. Be sure to protect your head and neck as you move to the bottom of the boat. Tuck into a ball and wait for the current to push you downriver.

Step 4: Beware the hydraulic.

If your raft gets stuck in a hydraulic (a very large hole with reverse water flow), it will try and surf your boat back and forth and probably flip you. It may randomly kick you out if you are lucky. If at all possible, use a paddle to grab some water outside the hydraulic or to push off a rock.

CAPSIZING AND RESCUE TIPS

▪ **If the raft flips, take care of your companions first, your raft second.**
Do a head count and make sure everyone is visible. Cold water could lead to hypothermia, so it is important to get everyone out of the water and back into the raft quickly. Energetic paddling will get the blood flowing and help warm up your crew.

▪ **If one of your passengers is thrown out of the raft, haul him in.**
If he is close to the raft, offer him a paddle to grab onto and move it so that he can grab onto the side of the raft. If he is farther away, toss him a throw bag. Instruct him to grab onto the rope and then turn his back to the boat with the rope over one shoulder. Pull him close to the boat. To get him into the boat, grab his lifejacket by each shoulder, bend your knees, and lean back, pulling him into the boat and on top of you.

▪ **If you are thrown out of the boat in heavy water and cannot swim to shore or get back to the raft, make sure you are on your back.**
Use your arms to help you steer where you want to go. Your feet should be pointed downstream. If you need to avoid an obstacle immediately, you may have to roll over on your stomach and actively swim to a safer area. If you have an opportunity to grab the raft or swim to shore, use it.

▪ **If you are out of the raft and caught in a hydraulic, tuck yourself into a ball.**
Ideally, the water will shoot you below the hydraulic and spit you out downstream.

HOW TO ESCAPE
ON HORSEBACK

Arwen (Liv Tyler): *If I can get across the river the power of my people will protect him . . .*
Aragorn (Viggo Mortensen): *Ride hard! Don't look back.*
    —*Lord of the Rings: The Fellowship of the Ring*

Women can dance backward and in high heels. They can also gallop on a horse, even when perched sidesaddle and weighed down with petticoats and a skirt. Helping a hobbit, rounding up desperados, and chasing down a mugger in the park are no sweat when you have a trusty steed. Rancher "Roudy" Roudebush advises that a good horse-woman takes care of her horse so it will take care of her when the time comes to evade pursuers. Besides protecting a hobbit and his ring, you will get a good workout, foil your foes, and look magnificent as the wind whips through your hair.

THE QUICK MOUNT

To jump on a horse from behind, the horse must be comfortable with the move. Your horse must be trained to stay still as you mount, or she should be tied to a post with a simple slipknot.

Step 1: Run toward the rear of the horse.

Do not sprint full speed. Just gain some momentum.

Step 2: Jump off from one leg and plant your hands on either side of the horse's haunches.

Plant your hands firmly on the horse's rear. This will tell the

Keep legs spread.

Plant hands on either side
of horse's haunches and push off
toward the saddle.

Secure horse to
a post.

Lift yourself onto the horse and catch the horn of the saddle.

horse that you are coming as well as allow you to vault up over her haunches.

Step 3: Spread your legs and lift yourself onto the horse.

As you continue to rise, press down with your hands—arms locked—so that your hands pass between your thighs as you pass over the tail. Push off toward the saddle and lift your hands up as your hips clear them.

Step 4: Land in the saddle and untie the horse.

Time your landing in the saddle so that you do not land on the horn. You may catch the horn with your hands to help bring your body into the seat. Untie the slipknot (if used) and begin to ride.

ESCAPE

Step 1: Ride quickly to the cover of trees or a desert canyon.

Get out of sight by riding to the closest cover of trees or canyon available. Initially, ride the horse as fast as she can go. Gauge your speed by how far off your pursuers are. If there is equal or greater distance between your pursuers and your nearest cover, slow your horse slightly to sustain her energy. If your pursuers are closer to you than you are to your cover, increase your speed as necessary.

Step 2: Find and stay on a trail.

Stay on the trail to avoid having to bushwhack or cut through trees. Horses naturally move faster and more comfortably on trails. If you are in unfamiliar territory, you may find a trail heading both away from and toward a water source.

Step 3: Lope your horse and ride to open ground if you have a sizeable lead.

Slow your horse to a fast walk by tugging slightly on the reins. Your pursuers will likely be racing to catch up with you and thus tiring out their horses. Steer your horse to a clearing, where she will be able to gallop quickly and unimpeded.

Step 4: Gallop back into the cover of trees.

You should now have a significant lead. Leave the trail and travel through dark timber to confuse and possibly lose your pursuers. As you travel off the path, look ahead and guide your horse around trees, rocks, or other obstacles.

Step 5: Take steps to avoid being tracked.

Even with a substantial lead, you can still be tracked. Use the following evasive techniques:

- Wrap your horse's hooves in burlap so that she covers her own tracks.
- Find a river and ride downstream. Avoid riding upstream, as turned-up mud and rocks may give away your position.
- Leave the stream and then loop back to it. This may lead your pursuers away from your path for some time.

HOW TO OUTRUN A TORNADO IN A CAR

Jo (Helen Hunt): *If it drops anywhere near us—*
Bill (Bill Paxton): *It's not gonna drop anywhere near us, it's gonna drop*
  right on us!
        —Twister

While it's good to explore your natural environs, don't mess with forces of nature (lest you wind up doing battle with witches and winged monkeys). A twister is a wily foe, and it can turn on you at any second. It can take the roof off your house. It can pick up your car and throw it around like a maraca. To outrun a tornado, get in the driver's seat and put serious distance between you and it. Storm chaser Roger Hill points out that this is not a time to stop and ask for directions. Don't get swept up in the moment; focus on one goal—making the twister appear smaller in your rearview mirror.

WHEN A TORNADO DROPS ON TOP OF YOU

The chances of a tornado dropping on top of you are less than the chances of getting struck by lightning. Your chances are greatly increased, however, if you are in "tornado alley," which runs from Texas north through to the Dakotas. It's a good idea to be on the lookout in twister-prone areas. Keep a compass in your car and be aware of the direction you are traveling.

Step 1: Recognize the signs of a tornado.

Be aware of the signs that you may be in a tornado drop zone:

- A "sickly" green- or black-colored sky

Use a crossroad to turn 90 degrees away from the tornado's path.

- Hail—the larger the hailstones, the more intense the storm
- A "strange quiet" immediately after a rain or hail storm
- Rotating and/or quickly moving clouds
- The sound of a "waterfall" or "rushing air" (indicating an approaching or developing tornado)
- Debris (branches, pieces of homes, trucks, cattle, or the like) falling from the sky
- An obvious funnel-shaped cloud

Step 2: Immediately head away from the storm.

Roll up your car windows, secure your sun or moon roof, and make sure your doors are shut tight. If you can, drive your car away from the direction of the storm. Use a crossroad or highway exit to turn 90 degrees away from its path. If you cannot determine its direction, drive on a westerly or southwesterly course (see note, below). Ideally, you should attempt to get *behind* the tornado. A tornado will usually move forward, not backward.

Note: Tornados may travel in any direction, but severe thunderstorms that become tornados move with or slightly away from the jet stream and more frequently move from southwest to northeast. Proceeding on a westerly or southwesterly course increases your chances of moving behind a storm.

Step 3: Drive as quickly as you can to get at least two miles away from the path of the tornado.

Tornados are generally about 50 to 100 yards wide when they begin, so once you're out of the drop zone (or behind the tornado), a two-mile barrier between you and the tornado should be sufficient.

Neo (Keanu Reeves): *Can you fly that thing?*
Trinity (Carrie-Anne Moss): *Not yet.*
Tank (Marcus Chong): *Operator.*
Trinity: *Tank, I need a pilot program for a V-212 helicopter.*
          —*The Matrix*

You're one tough, multi-talented chick, so it's no surprise that you can calmly climb behind the controls of a failing chopper. Like playing a piano, flying a helicopter employs all of your limbs, and it's challenging to operate the controls simultaneously. So if a pilot program cannot be instantaneously loaded into your brain, keep a clear head and make smooth, gradual movements to land your aircraft. Bring your innate grace and competence to the job at hand and follow the instructions of pilots Randy York and John Moore. You'll be on the ground in no time.

Note: Controls, switches, and equipment vary from aircraft to aircraft.

ENGINE FAILURE

The engine drives the transmission, which drives the rotor system. If the engine quits due to mechanical failure or lack of gas, you must auto-rotate.

Step 1: Push the collective down to take pitch out of the main rotor blades.
  You will begin an immediate descent.

Step 2: Keep the helicopter in trim (i.e., a straight direction) by pushing forward slightly on the right pedal.

HELICOPTER BASICS

- **THE CYCLIC** is the control stick in front of the pilot, usually mounted on the floor of the helicopter, that is held in the right hand. It controls the main rotor blades on top of the helicopter, the attitude (i.e., direction), and the airspeed of the aircraft.

- **THE COLLECTIVE PITCH CONTROL,** also a stick, is located to the left of the pilot and should be held in the left hand. It collectively adds pitch to (i.e., changes the angle of) the main rotor blades.

- **THE THROTTLE** is mounted on the forward end of the collective pitch lever in the form of a motorcycle-type twist grip. It regulates the rotor RPM. When twisted toward you, it decreases RPM; when twisted away from you, it increases RPM.

- **THE PEDALS** control the pitch of the tail rotor blades. They allow the helicopter to turn left or right. When the right pedal is pushed forward, the helicopter will turn to the right. When the left pedal is pushed, it will turn left.

Use the right pedal if your copter is manufactured in the U.S. If it's made in France, use the left pedal.

Step 3: Adjust the cyclic until your speed reaches 60 knots.

If you are going faster than 60 knots, pull back on the cyclic until you reach this airspeed. If you are going slower, push forward on the cyclic to increase your airspeed. At this point, the main rotor blades will operate like a pinwheel, with the upward air causing the blades to turn and cushion the landing.

Step 4: Identify an appropriate landing spot.

Look for a flat area; avoid power lines, water, and areas dense with foliage or people.

Step 5: Shut the fuel off.

Close the fuel shut-off valve or switch. Switch off the booster pumps, generator, and inverter.

Step 6: Land the helicopter.

When you are 100 feet above the ground, decelerate the aircraft by pulling back on the cyclic until you reach a speed of 10 knots. At an altitude of 20 feet, push the cyclic forward to level the aircraft. When you are 5 feet above ground, pull up on the collective to cushion your landing. If you feel you are descending rapidly, pull up quickly. If you feel you are floating in the wind, pull up slowly. Note that you only have one chance to do this perfectly.

Step 7: Once on the ground, lower the collective to the full-down position.

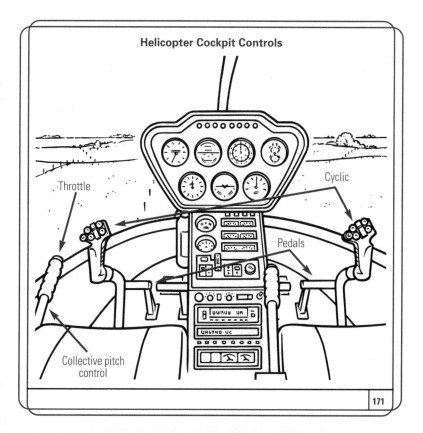

Helicopter Cockpit Controls

Throttle

Cyclic

Pedals

Collective pitch control

LOSS OF TAIL ROTOR AUTHORITY

If the tail totor is damaged in any way, your pedals may be useless.

Step 1: Maintain forward air speed.

Use the cyclic to maintain a forward speed of 60 knots. You will create wind that will cause the aircraft to "weather vane," or point into the wind.

Step 2: Locate an appropriate landing spot.

Look for a flat area such as a pasture or maybe even a runway; avoid power lines, water, and areas dense with foliage or people. You want to "run the aircraft on" and make a slide-on landing with your forward airspeed.

Step 3: Gradually decrease your altitude and airspeed.

Simultaneously lower the collective until you reach an altitude of 20 feet, push down on the right pedal to reduce the torque, and pull back with the cyclic to slow the airspeed to 60 knots. Gradually reduce the altitude to 1 to 2 feet above the ground and slow your airspeed to 30 knots.

Step 4: Make small heading corrections by rolling off the throttle to turn the helicopter to the left or rolling on the throttle to turn to the right.

Maintain the heading in the direction the helicopter is moving, and land the helicopter by running it on or sliding it on (much like an airplane would land—on landing gear while moving forward). As you make surface contact, pull back slightly on the cyclic to keep the helicopter light on its skids and to gradually slow it down.

Step 5: When the helicopter stops, lower the collective to its full-down position.

HOW TO WIN A CHASE ACROSS ROOFTOPS

Jen Yu (Zhang Ziyi): *Who am I? I am . . . I am the Invincible Sword Goddess, armed with the incredible Green Destiny. Be you Li or Southern Crane, lower your head and ask for mercy. I am the desert dragon. I leave no trace. Today I fly over Eu-Mei. Tomorrow . . . I'll kick over Wudan Mountain!*
    —Crouching Tiger, Hidden Dragon

It's a proven fact that women are nimble. With your low center of gravity and years of ballet training and/or the tightrope skills you picked up at Club Med, you can quickly learn to traverse rooftops and treetops. Whether fleeing pursuers after lifting a legendary sword or in hot pursuit of the enemy, follow the advice of urban gymnast ArEe of Le Parkour Clan and you will assuredly out-scamper your male foe. Your adversary might not have two left feet, but you can bet he doesn't have your innate grace—or the proper footwear (see "It's All About the Shoes," p. 16).

BASIC MOVES

You should master several basic moves, whether maneuvering in the city, an abandoned warehouse, or across suburban Chinese rooftops.

Crossing

Use this move to proceed quickly from point A to point B, when a moveable obstacle like a garbage can or thin bamboo tree is in your path.

Step 1: Run toward the obstacle.

Gauge the size of the obstacle and adjust your speed accordingly. For taller or wider obstacles, run faster. For shorter or narrower obstacles, run slower. Generally, the larger the obstacle, the more momentum you need.

Step 2: Grasp the obstacle.

Use one or two hands to secure it. The larger or heavier the obstacle, the better the grasp you need. Grip the object firmly, but lightly enough to let go once you have cleared it.

Step 3: Clear the obstacle up, down, or to the side.

Use the "natural" flow of the object's position to clear it from your path. If you are clearing a garbage can that is leaning to the right, push it on its "natural" path down and to the right. If you are clearing a bamboo tree that is leaning away from you, bend the tree down as you run over it to clear it underneath you.

Jumps

Use these moves to proceed quickly upward or downward from point A to point B.

TO JUMP UP ONTO A ROOFTOP OR WALL:

Step 1: Run quickly toward your target.

Step 2: Leap upward off your dominant foot.

Step 3: Use your non-dominant foot to propel you upward by landing it on the vertical surface of the target.

Plant your foot firmly on the wall and press upward to continue upward.

Step 4: Grasp the roof or wall with both hands and continue upward.

To jump onto a rooftop or wall, plant your foot firmly on the wall,
grasp the roof with both hands, and continue upward.

TO JUMP ACROSS A ROOF TO ANOTHER ROOF:

Step 1: Run to the end of the roof and leap off your dominant foot toward the target roof.

Step 2: Bring your legs together as you sail through the air. Lead with your feet so that you will be prepared for landing.

Step 3: Keep your arms out to your sides and wave them in small circles to propel you forward. Bring your arms in front of you as you approach your landing.

Step 4: Absorb the impact of the landing by planting your feet firmly on the ground.

Step 5: Let your knees bend forward as you tuck your head into your chest and roll over your leading shoulder.

TO JUMP FROM A ROOF TO THE GROUND:

Do not jump more than one story down.

Step 1: Spot a clear landing area, free from obstructions, on the ground below you.

Step 2: Jump down from the rooftop or wall and toward your target.

Step 3: Keep your eyes on your landing zone and your legs extended straight at the target.

Step 4: Keep your arms and hands in front of you, slightly bent at about shoulder height.

Step 5: As above, let your body absorb the impact of the landing, roll, and then continue to run.

Marshall Flinkman (Kevin Weisman) to Sydney Bristow (Jennifer Garner): *If you're stuck in the ducts when the rocket launches, then, well, boom. And I'd miss you.*
—*Alias*

Action heroines never need someone to light a fire under them to get them motivated, so launching a fireball in your direction is, well, overkill. Of course you would be on your guard against fiery explosions when caught in a war zone, but these days you should be alert at all times. A bazooka, for example, can be launched anywhere, even in the kitchen of a 5-star restaurant. If the enemy is polite, he'll wait until the dessert course, but don't count on it. Excuse yourself, fold your napkin on your chair, and run like hell. The following instructions come from stuntwoman Debbie Kahana.

Step 1: Determine where the fireball will be coming from.

Listen for an initial "boom" or "whistle" that indicates an explosive device is headed in your direction.

Step 2: Turn away from the potential explosion and run.

Determine its path, turn your back to the impending explosion, and run as quickly as you can.

Step 3: Feel the explosion to know when it has hit.

You will feel the heat and pressure of the blast at your back.

Step 4: Jump as far as you can upward and forward.

The shockwave may help you gain distance as you jump.
Immediately jump off your dominant foot. DO NOT stop running

To outrun a fireball:

1. Jump upward and forward off your dominant foot.

2. Bend at the waist with your shoulder forwardmost.

3. Hit the ground palms first.

4. Roll onto your leading shoulder.

to jump from both feet. Keep your forward momentum to gain distance in the air as well as on the ground.

Step 5: Position yourself for maximum distance and landing.
Stretch your body out as if you were flying through the air, hands first, with your head between your outstretched arms. As you begin to come down, bend forward at the waist and kick your legs over your head. Bend your arms so that your hands are tucked, palms out, near your shoulders. This will shift your body so that your shoulder is the forwardmost point of your trajectory. (Your roll will be diagonal across your body while you move in a straight line.)

Step 6: Hit the ground palms first, and tuck your body to roll.
Point your fingers at one another and raise your arms slightly in front of you to form a circle. Absorb the impact of the landing by slightly bending your elbows. Plant your hands on your non-dominant side and continue your momentum by rolling onto your dominant shoulder. Tuck your body into a ball as you roll over your shoulder, across your spine, and onto your opposite hip. Let your head "go with the roll": Keep it firmly tucked slightly forward and between your shoulders.

Step 7: Continue to roll until you have reached shelter or have slowed your momentum and the fireball subsides.
Your points of impact as you roll are as follows: hands, forearm, outside elbow, leading shoulder, opposite hip, knees, hands, and so on. Roll to shelter (behind a dumpster, into a dumbwaiter, or the like), or stand up when your momentum has slowed and run to safety.

Every action heroine knows that the handbag houses vital everyday items that—in the right combination—are an arsenal of tools for virtually any situation.

Nail File

A metal nail file has multiple uses for the manicured heroine on the move. A double-sided file may be used:
- As a tool for eye-gouging
- To file one or two nails to a sharp point
- As a lock pick, in combination with a bobby pin

Lipstick

The lush-lipped heroine may carry several tubes of lipstick. Any shade may be used:
- For writing messages on mirrors or glass
- As a camouflaged listening device, in combination with a remote sensor
- To create fake bruises and cuts

Perfume

A small aerosol bottle of perfume may be used to attract the attention of your enemies and, in addition:
- As a blinding spray
- As a flame thrower or light soldering tool, in combination with a lighter
- To sterilize a wound

Compact

A compact may serve:
- As a signal mirror
- As eyes "in the back of your head"
- When broken, as a blade or sharp implement
- To provide powder when dusting for fingerprints (it will adhere to the prints); if blown, compact powder can also temporarily blind an assailant or detect a field of laser beams
- Cream blush in a compact can be used to take an imprint of a key

Cigarettes

Though best not to use addictively, cigarettes of any brand may be used:

- To buy time (as in, "May I have one last smoke?")
- As a burning weapon
- To identify whether your suspect is left-handed or right-handed when he leans in to light your cigarette

Scarf

A tightly woven yet elegant scarf may protect your neck from a pressure point attack. You may also use a scarf:

- As a tourniquet or field bandage
- As a blindfold
- As a temporary restraint

Panty liner

Good for many emergency situations, the panty liner can do double or triple duty:

- As a bandage
- As a writing surface for jotting down notes
- As a sleep mask—after you've saved the world

Tampon

A feminine protection essential, the tampon has additional uses:

- The cotton roll can absorb a drink or other liquid for analysis
- The tube can be used to hide money, microfilm, or loose jewels

Nail polish

The well-manicured action heroine can use her jungle-red polish:

- To write short notes or small signs
- To secure knots or frayed edges

Gum

An excellent breath freshener, gum can add a convincing touch when working undercover as a high school student or "working girl," but can also be used:

- To rig a door alarm
- To jam a lock
- To take an imprint of a fingerprint or key

- To secure a listening device in a hidden spot
- To retrieve small items from a grate or other tight spot, when affixed to the end of a string or stick
- To secure a DNA sample, when offered to your opponent

Lotion

Hand lotion provides essential moisturizing at all times, but can also be used:
- To lubricate your hands to remove handcuffs
- To loosen knots

Matches

A matchbook can remind you of that romantic dinner with the debonair enemy you duped, or it can be used:
- To set off a smoke detector or fire alarm
- To dust for prints (by grinding several burnt carbon tips)
- To destroy incriminating papers
- To mask your perfume as you leave the room

Diaphragm

An action heroine never lets her libido get the best of her, but a diaphragm can be used:
- To plug a drain or leak
- As a makeshift funnel (when rolled up)
- To get a firm grip on a stuck radiator or gas can cap

Condom

You can momentarily distract your foe by flashing the little foil packet, but you can also use a condom:
- As a flotation device (blow up a 12-pack and tie them together for support)
- To make a slingshot (use two condoms tied together)
- To hold water or other fluid samples for analysis

With a whole lot of hairspray and a little ingenuity, any action heroine can be ready to charm an Intergalactic smuggler or take on the mother of all aliens.

The Farrah

Works best on: Long, layered hair with a steep angle around the face
Product: Volumizing mousse, aerosol hairspray
Step 1: Work mousse into wet hair. Rough-dry hair until it is approximately 85 percent dry.
Step 2: With a medium or large round metal brush, roll sections of hair away from face. Direct hot hair dryer on brush as you continuously roll hair onto it. Repeat until each section is dry. In the back, roll sections of hair down and under, and dry with the same method.
Step 3: When hair is completely dry, flip your head over and spray the underside. Flip it into place and spray, paying extra attention to the sides. If your hair is too stiff, lightly run a brush or your fingers through the hair to soften.

The Wonder Woman

Works best on: Long hair past the shoulders, either blunt or slightly layered
Product: Hairspray
Step 1: Begin with dry hair. To add extra volume at the crown, tease the top and sides with a rattail comb.
Step 2: Spray or spritz hair and gently smooth over into a bubble shape.
Step 3: Roll hair from the temple down in hot rollers. Leave in for 5 to 10 minutes, or until rollers are cool.
Step 4: Remove rollers and run fingers or a widetooth comb through curls to soften.
Step 5: Place tiara on top of head.
Step 6: Finish with a laminating spray for extra Amazon shine.

The Ripley

Works best on: Thick, wavy or curly hair
Product: Styling gel
Prep: This style features a 90-degree haircut, in which all of your hair is cut the same distance from your scalp. Simply apply a light gel through the hair and scrunch it with your hands as it air-dries.

The Princess Leia
Long-hair version

Works best on: Blunt-cut long hair, at least four to five inches beyond shoulder

Product: Hairspray, and lots of it

Prep: You will need to make a pair of ratts. Loosely stuff a sheer knee-high stocking (in a shade that generally matches your hair color), with batting or cotton. Feed the closed end into the open end, thereby making a doughnut shape. Repeat procedure to make a pair.

Step 1: Part hair down the middle of your scalp, from forehead to nape.

Step 2: Make a ponytail on either side of your head above each ear. Secure with an elastic band.

Step 3: Thread a ponytail through the ratt so that it sits right against your head.

Step 4: Taking a rattail comb, section out small pieces from the ponytail in turn and wrap the hair over the ratt.

Step 5: Tuck the ends of your hair underneath the ratt and secure hair all around the ratt with bobby pins.

Step 6: Repeat on the other side.

Step 7: When finished, spray liberally with hairspray.

Shoulder-length version

Works best on: Shoulder-length hair, blunt cut or slightly layered

Product: Pomade, hairspray

Step 1: Apply a light pomade to wet hair and rough blow dry.

Step 2: Part hair down the middle of your scalp, from forehead to nape.

Step 3: Make a ponytail on either side of your head, right above the ear. Secure with an elastic band.

Step 4: Loosely braid each ponytail and secure with elastic bands at the ends.

Step 5: Envisioning a cinnamon bun, wrap braid around itself, pinning with bobby pins as you go.

Step 6: Tuck the end of the braid under the bun and secure with bobby pins.

Step 7: Using a rattail comb, go into the braid bun and backcomb it in places to give it volume.

Step 8: Set style with hairspray.

Action Heroine Hairstyles

The Farrah: Blow-dry hair away from face. Hair should be soft and full of volume.

The Wonder Woman: Place tiara atop head for finishing touch.

The Ripley: Apply light gel and scrunch hair as it dries.

The Princess Leia: Wrap braid around itself to form a "cinnamon bun." Set style with spray.

CHAPTER 1—TOUGH CHICK SKILLS

How to Win a High-Speed Chase in High Heels and a Bustier—Danielle Burgio is a stuntwoman who has worked on *The Matrix Reloaded*, *The Matrix 3*, *Daredevil*, *Angel*, and *Birds of Prey*. She is "Gear Girl" for the TBS television series *Worst-Case Scenario*. *It's All About the Shoes*—Dr. Gregory Kaufman is a podiatrist currently practicing in Englewood, Rockleigh, and Palisades Park, New Jersey. He is affiliated with Englewood Hospital and Medical Center in Englewood, New Jersey, and Holy Name Hospital in Teaneck, New Jersey.

How to Navigate a Roomful of Laser Beams—Nina Vought currently teaches Yoga and Theatre at Westminster College in Salt Lake City. She has been active in drama, dance, martial arts, and yoga for nearly two decades.

How to Pop a Nose Wheelie on a Motorcycle—Ken Kelley owns and operates the Adrenalin Crew (www.adrenalinecrew.com), the entertainment industry's leading motorcycle company for stunt work in video and film.

How to Go Toe to Toe with the Guys in Your Special Unit—"Fastball" is a protection officer for a very high level diplomatic post. She graduated from the Center for Advanced Security Studies at the top of her (mostly male) class.

How to Drink Someone Under the Table—Nick Parkin has tended bar for 15 years in Utah, Arizona, South Carolina, and New York City. He can always be found on one side of the bar or the other.

How to Surf a Barreling Wave—Kathy Jo Anderson is an inductee to the East Coast Surf Legends Hall of Fame. Kathy and her daughter Missy founded the Betty Series (www.thebettyseries.com) competition and clinics designed for females only in 2001. Lisa Wakely Muir has been surfing for 33 years and was inducted into the East Coast Surf Legends Hall of Fame in 2002.

How to Rescue a Drowning Swimmer—Linda Delzeit-McIntyre has been training lifeguards since 1977 and is the aquatics director at Los Angeles Trade Technical College. She is an instructor and trainer for the American Red Cross in Lifeguard Training, Water Safety, First Aid, and CPR.

How to Fend Off the Undead—Bishop Sean Manchester has specialized in the ministry of exorcism for three decades and is acknowledged by many as Britain's foremost authority on demonology (including vampirology) and exorcism. He is responsible for over half a dozen books and several television documentary films. Simon Brind (Count Von Sexbat) has seen an average number of B-movie horror flicks and was once thrown out of a pub in North London for trying to stake a vampire role-player with a broken pool cue.

How to Outwit a Sasquatch—Richard Noll is a Bigfoot Research Organization curator in the State of Washington. He is considered an expert in casting animal tracks in the field and has been involved with Sasquatch research since 1979.

How to Give Birth Under Pressure—Nan H. Troiano, RN, MSN, is codirector of Critical Care Obstetrics at Jefferson Medical College of Thomas Jefferson University, Department of Obstetrics and Gynecology, Division of Maternal Fetal Medicine, in Philadelphia.

How to Protect Your Child from a Ferocious Beast—Russ Smith is the Curator of Reptiles at the Los Angeles Zoo.

CHAPTER 2—BEAUTY SKILLS

How to Turn Yourself into a Hottie in Five Minutes or Less—Rachel Hayes is the beauty director of *Cosmopolitan* magazine.

How to Own the Dance Floor—Cynthia Fleming has served as choreographer for a variety of theater productions, trade shows, and tributes. She performed in *A Chorus Line* in the Broadway, international, and national companies. *How to Tango*—Cynthia Fleming. *How to Dance Like a Maniac*—Cynthia Fleming. *How to Striptease*—Shannon Cromwell has been a stripper and currently specializes in amateur and theme pornography, erotic photography, and web design; her website is sinisher.com.

How to Hook a Millionaire—Patti Stanger is the CEO and owner of the Millionaire's Club, a dating service for millionaires (www.millionairesclub123.com).

How to Turn a Man into a Sex Pawn—Mistress Mimi Divine, Diva Veronica Bound, Passion, Goddess Destiny Kaine, and Domina Barbie are dominatrixes at the Olde English Chambers in Philadelphia.

How to Seduce the Enemy—Carol Queen, Ph.D., is the staff sexologist at Good Vibrations in San Francisco. She is an author and sex educator who has written and edited several books, including *Exhibitionism for the Shy* and *Real Live Nude Girl: Chronicles of Sex-Positive Culture* (www.carolqueen.com). *Clothing Guaranteed to Distract the Enemy*—John Columbo is the co-owner of Forbidden Planett, a Philadelphia shop specializing in vintage clothing and fetish gear, and Miss Dior's Tramp, a shop specializing in vintage and custom-designed lingerie.

CHAPTER 3—BRAIN SKILLS

How to Profile a Serial Killer—John A. Dicke, Psy.D., J.D., is a clinical and forensic psychologist specializing in diagnosing attachment, trauma, dissociative disorders, and psychopathy. He has provided forensic testimony in numerous serial killer and rapist cases, and regularly conducts competency and sanity evaluations. Shawn Engbrecht is one of the world's top protection officers. When he is not on operational assignment all over the world, he is one of the instructors at the Center for Advanced Security Studies, specializing in the training and placement of world-class bodyguards.

How to Eavesdrop from a Distance—Linda Kessler, M.A., CCC-S, has been a speech and language pathologist for almost 40 years. Linda is currently Coordinator of Adult Communication Services at the League for the Hard of Hearing in New York City.

How to Investigate Your Spouse/Lover—Carmen Naimish is a Licensed Private Investigator in the State of California and is the founder of Datesmart.com, featured in numerous publications and TV and radio programs in the U.S., Canada, and Europe. She has been solving crimes of the heart since 1997.

How to Survive as a Mob Wife—Rick Porrello is a veteran cop with mob roots and author of *The Rise and Fall of the Cleveland Mafia* and *To Kill the Irishman—The War That Crippled the Mafia.*

How to Keep Your Cool Under Interrogation—Detective Chip Morgan is a criminal polygraph examiner with the Boise Police Department. Detective Morgan has shared his training and expertise with others in the law enforcement arena.

How to Outwit a Band of Home Intruders—Chris McGoey, a.k.a. the Crime Doctor, works from San Francisco and Los Angeles. He is a 30-year veteran in security management and crime prevention and the internationally known webmaster of www.crimedoctor.com

How to Go Undercover—Dennis Spillman was a uniformed Philadelphia police officer for eight years and worked undercover for two years. He was also a detective for the Philadelphia district attorney and investigated insurance fraud. *How to Go Undercover as a Beauty Queen*—Kate Wilson has competed in beauty pageants for twelve years, most recently holding the Miss Philadelphia and Miss Midstate title in the Miss America system. *How to Go Undercover as a Prostitute*—"Pleasure" has been a working girl for three years. She currently works at the Moonlight Bunnyranch in Nevada. *How to Go Undercover as a Man*—Jo-El Schult is a drag king who performs in the Bay area under the name Rusty Hips.

How to Maintain a Secret Identity—Elvin W. Keith spent 23 years in the FBI as an agent specializing in counterintelligence. He had previously spent six years in the USMC as an officer and is a Vietnam veteran; Shawn Engbrecht.

How to Survive in the Wild—"Mountain" Mel Deweese is a retired USN Survival Evasion Resistance Escape Instructor who has taught more than 100,000 students and has more than 30 years of survival training experience. He is the owner of Nature Knowledge in Grand Junction, Colorado (www.youwillsurvive.com). *How to Deal with a Gorilla in the Mist*—Andy Baker is Vice President for Animal Programs at the Philadelphia Zoo.

CHAPTER 4—BRAWN SKILLS

How to Win a Catfight—Danielle Burgio. *How to Take a Hit in the Boobs*—Known as the "Zion Lion," Jill Matthews was the Junior Flyweight World Champion in 1998, as well as the first woman to win the Golden Gloves in 1995. She is also featured in an HBO Boxing Playstation video game.

How to Choke a Man with Your Bare Thighs—Robert Hodgkin has been studying Dan Zan Ryu Jujitsu since 1982, and is currently a 4th-degree black belt with the American Judo and Jujitsu Federation.

How to Subdue Your Opponent with a Whip—Danielle Burgio.

How to Fight with Your Hands Cuffed—Shawn Engbrecht.

How to Knock Out a Man with a Running Wall Kick—Carrie Wong is a former Forms and Weapons National Champion. She operates and instructs at the White Lotus Kung Fu System in Northridge, California.

How to Disarm a Knife-Wielding Killer—Sensei Debbie Hamilton is a 2nd-degree black belt and the chief instructor and owner of the Naples Academy of Martial Arts in Naples, Florida (naplesama@earthlink.net or www.amadojo.com).

CHAPTER 5—ESCAPE SKILLS

How to Fake Your Own Death—Elvin W. Keith; Shawn Engbrecht.

How to Escape When Kidnapped—Larry J. Chavez, B.A., M.P.A., is a 31-year law enforcement veteran, former senior hostage negotiator of a large police agency, and graduate of the FBI Hostage Negotiations School at Quantico, Virginia. His expertise has been featured on national television (www.workplace-violence.com).

How to Fend Off a Sexually Harassing Trucker—Andrew Netschay is the founder of Confrontation Management Systems. He is considered an authority on negotiation, confrontation, and safety strategy. Dawn Rodriguez is a four-year over-the-road truck driver, mom, trucker's wife, and writer for Layover.com's Women in Trucking (www.layover.com/driverscorner/womenintrucking).

How to Maneuver a Raft Down Class V+ Rapids—Heather Ewing is the co-owner of Barker-Ewing River Trips in Jackson Hole, Wyoming.

How to Escape on Horseback—Thomas Alta "Roudy" Roudebush is a cowboy and dude rancher in Colorado. He has been running horseback trips for nearly 30 years.

How to Outrun a Tornado in a Car—Roger Hill has been chasing tornados since 1986, during which time he has intercepted over 200 tornados. He runs a storm chasing tour company (www.stormchase.net) and works on numerous National Severe Storms Laboratory projects.

How to Land a Failing Helicopter—Randy York is the owner of West Florida

Helicopters in St. Petersburg, Florida. With more than 16,000 hours of flight time and 35 years of experience, he has been a commercial airplane and helicopter pilot, flight instructor, and FAA helicopter flight examiner, and he served two tours in Vietnam. John Moore is the owner of Island Express, a helicopter service on Catalina Island, California. He has been flying since 1967 and has flown helicopters in Vietnam and Alaska.

How to Win a Chase Across Rooftops—ArEe is the leader of the urban gymnasts' Parkour Clan Group (www.parkourklan.fr.st) and has been practicing Le Parkour for 3 years.

How to Outrun a Fireball—Debbie Kahana began her stunt career at age 8 in Los Angeles. She has worked on several major motion pictures, including *The Towering Inferno*, *Earthquake*, and *Lethal Weapon III*. She owns and operates "Stunts Are Us"—a non-profit stunt training facility in Kenosha, WI (www.stuntsareus.com).

Appendix B: Action Heroine Hairstyles—Buddy Eberwein has been a stylist for ten years. He has trained at Toni & Guy in London, done platform work for Fudge at IBS in New York, and taught advanced hair cutting technique.

ABOUT THE AUTHORS

Jennifer Worick is the co-author of the *New York Times* bestseller *The Worst-Case Scenario Survival Handbook: Dating & Sex* (Chronicle). Armed with expertise in the subject area, she frequently does battle with the opposite sex, usually winning and occasionally losing (on purpose). Still looking for a golden lasso that forces men to spill the beans, she is also the author of *Nancy Drew's Guide to Life* (Running Press), the co-author of *The Art of Belly Dancing* (Running Press), and the co-author of *The Rebound Book* and *My Fabulous Life* (Chronicle). She lives in Philadelphia, where she undergoes a rigorous action heroine training regime almost daily.

Joe Borgenicht is the co-author of *The Action Hero's Handbook* (Quirk). As an action hero in training, he has realized that every hero has his heroine (who's better to watch on the big screen anyway). He hopes that the future holds more heroines in everyday life, and in phone booths and changing rooms around the world. He is also the co-author of *The Baby Owner's Manual* (Quirk), *Doggy Days* (Ten Speed), and *Mom Always Said, "Don't Play Ball in the House," and Other Stuff We Learned from TV* (Chilton). He lives in Salt Lake City with his heroine-wife, Melanie, his mini-me son, Jonah, and his faithful watchdog, Satie.

ACKNOWLEDGMENTS

Jennifer Worick would like to thank the following people: Mindy "Wonder Woman" Brown, for being patient while she finished that last #@%^& skill; the Amazing Borgenicht Brothers, for their humor and heroic profiles; and Bryn Ashburn, Colette Eddy, Josh Freely, Liesa Goins, Peter Gwin, Kate Hatem, Robin Hommel, Stanka Luna, Drucie McDaniel, Janice and Drew Peterson, Josh Piven, Susan Portnoy, Jason Rekulak, Ted Schmitz, Frances Soo Ping Chow, Alex Stadler, Kerry Sturgill, and Jared Von Arx for their kind help and support in making this project happen. She cannot thank enough the talented experts in this book who so generously offered their time and expertise. Finally, she would like to give a shout out to her personal action heroines who save her life every day—Alison, Kerry, Melissa, Sacha, Elizabeth, Fil, Mary, Erin, Larissa, Mel, Annie, Lil, Pat, and her mom, Judy.

Joe Borgenicht would like to thank all of the experts who lent their training and invaluable experience to this book; his co-author, Jennifer Worick, who was born to write this book; his editor, "Downtown" Mindy Brown, whose pen is mightier than any large man sitting next to her on a plane clutching a stuffed animal; and his brother, Dave, who IS (and will always BE) somebody. Thanks also to Bryn, Frances, Larry, Quirk Books, and Big Apple Pizzeria. Big love to all the heroines who inspired this manual: Angelina, Karen, J, Lynda, Catherine, Sarah Michelle, Lindsay, Carmen, Kate, Gillian, Sigourney, Sandra, Jennifer, Demi, Jamie Lee (and her sister, Kelly), Julia, Linda, Gwyneth, Jodie, Edie, Sharon, Daryl, Michelle, Cameron, Drew, Lucy, Ziyi, Neve, Ashley, Geena, Susan, Meryl, Liv, Carrie, Anne, Carrie-Anne, and both Heathers. Finally—and most thankfully—Joe would like to acknowledge his beautiful wife and son, for every day.